THE WORLD-CONQUERING FICTION

A critique of the Christian claim that Christ's death on the Cross provides salvation for a 'lost' humankind

John Bracht

THE WORLD-CONQUERING FICTION
A Critique of the Christian Claim that Christ's Death on the Cross Provides Salvation for a 'Lost' Humankind

Copyright © 2018 John L. Bracht. All rights reserved. Except for brief quotations in critical publications or reviews, no part of this book may be reproduced in any manner without prior written permission from the publisher. Write: Permissions, Wipf and Stock Publishers, 199 W. 8th Ave., Suite 3, Eugene, OR 97401.

First published in 2016 by Barrallier Books Pty Ltd, trading as Echo Books

Resource Publications
An Imprint of Wipf and Stock Publishers
199 W. 8th Ave., Suite 3
Eugene, OR 97401

www.wipfandstock.com

PAPERBACK ISBN: 978-1-4982-2034-7
HARDCOVER ISBN: 978-1-4982-2033-0
EBOOK ISBN: 978-1-4982-2035-4

Manufactured in the U.S.A.   01/26/18

*'We will not make common cause with
the world-conquering fiction of Christian dogma,
because (however much a fact), it* is *a fiction'*
—Franz Rosenzweig (1886–1929)

CONTENTS

Introduction	vii
The 'Good News'?	1
Two Testaments two Different Bibles	7
The 'Fall' and Human 'lostness'	19
Down the Rabbit Hole—Part 1	35
Down the Rabbit Hole—Part 2	57
Engaging with a Liberal Theologian – John Hick	77
The Twilight of Atheism?	91
Who Speaks for God?	103
Monster or handbag?	131
The Man behind the Veil	149
'God is plain to them'?	169
Summing Up	177
Notes	187
Bibliography	197
Index	203

Introduction

The grand, unique claim of the Christian religion is that it alone has the answer to the human 'plight', which is that all people are born into a state of 'lostness', and are, from the very beginning estranged from God. They live their lives, however happily in human terms, outside of God's will and real purpose for their lives. When and if they die outside of God's grace and salvation, they will enter an eternal state of separation from God. The solution to this terrible plight is the saving death of Jesus Christ on the cross. Anyone who accepts the sacrifice of Christ's death on his behalf, is granted forgiveness of sins and reconciliation with God. He or she will be 'saved' from God's judgment and wrath and given the promise of eternal life in heaven. This is the message, the 'good news' of the 'Gospel' which Christianity has been sharing with the world for 2,000 years. It has obviously had great success in propagating the message, because Christianity today is the largest religion on Earth.

But what if Christianity's grand and unique claim is false, a chimera? The definition of chimera means a thing which is hoped for but is illusory or impossible to achieve. What if Christianity's central, most fundamental doctrine could be described in those terms, so that the doctrine appears in all its naked absurdity as Christianity's weakest, most vulnerable point—

its Achilles heel? What if 'the Great Agnostic' Robert Ingersoll was correct in the Nineteenth Century when he said: 'The Christian religion rests upon the doctrine of the Atonement. If this doctrine is without foundation, the fabric fails; and it is without foundation, for it is repugnant to justice and mercy'.1 I am not trying to suggest something new or original. The Christian doctrine of salvation (soteriology) has been questioned and debated within the Church almost from the very beginning of Church history. During the last two or three hundred years at least, it has been seriously questioned as a way of understanding the death and teachings of Jesus. The people doing the questioning are not enemies of religion or 'new atheists', they are Christian theologians.

Does the Christian doctrine of salvation make sense? I hesitate to ask the question in that form because most believers know only too well that faith isn't supposed to make sense in a human, rational way. It is God's revealed truth, the 'mystery of faith', and it can only be understood through faith. That response however, has long ceased to be acceptable to most thinking people. If understanding this message is what my eternal destiny depends on, then I ought to be able to understand it. But not only is the doctrine incomprehensible, it is reprehensible. By that I mean that if there really were a God who wants to 'save' us, then this particular theory of salvation would put him in a very bad light. He would hardly be the loving, Heavenly Father he is reported to be.

This critique of the Christian doctrine of salvation is twofold: first to state in the clearest possible terms what the Christian doctrine of atonement or salvation is, with the expectation that seen in its stark, essential form, it will startle and bewilder rather than console or inspire. I will make some reference to Jewish writers who, historically, have never accepted the doctrine of the Christian Atonement, and who continue today to consider it 'absurd and immoral', 'repugnant to justice and mercy', 'unethical and unbelievable.'

Secondly, by engaging with a range of theologians—fundamentalist and liberal, I want to demonstrate that the doctrine is highly implausible, even incoherent. It ought to become increasingly evident that the more Christian theologians explain their view of salvation, the deeper the hole of incomprehensibility they dig. We are living at a time in history when the depths of real mystery (as opposed to divine mysteries) are being plumbed with ever-greater success. At the same time there is a growing and justified scepticism of the concocted mysteries, such as the Atonement of Christ, that have always been the stock-and-trade of religion. We seem to be in the midst of a paradigm shift in our perception of the 'truth' that is a real shaking of our inherited religious traditions.

Christian theologian Alister McGrath, echoes the thought of Robert Ingersoll, though with a different intention:

> The doctrine of justification (Christian explanation for how salvation works) fulfils a crucial role. It is the articulus stantis et cadentis ecclesiae, the 'article by which the church stands or falls.' The Christian Church takes its stand against a disbelieving world on the basis of the firm and constant belief that God acted in the death and resurrection of Jesus Christ to achieve something that will remain of permanent significance to human beings, so long as they walk the face of this planet knowing that they must die ... If this belief is false, the Christian faith must be recognized as a delusion—a deeply satisfying delusion, to be sure, but a delusion none the less.[2]

Contrast this statement with that of Lewis A. Hart, an early Twentieth century Jewish theologian:

> Surely, if Jesus were a God, and if the Almighty had intended that the people of Israel should worship Jesus as their God, their Lord and their Saviour, He would have said so in language as plain and unmistakable as that of any of the Ten Commandments; in words so plain that there could be no debate and no possibility of mistake about them. In a matter of such supreme importance as the salvation of souls, surely the Almighty would have instructed the Israelites, His chosen people and his witnesses, in a manner as clear and precise—nay, in a manner even more precise and clear than He used in matters pertaining to their moral and material welfare.[3]

Having been until recently a Christian minister, I believe I can give some helpful insights into what Christians say about their religion's offer of salvation and at the same time examine why all defences of this doctrine are inadequate and increasingly incomprehensible to most nonbelievers—not to mention thousands of questioning Christians. One of the common complaints of Christian theologians is that the 'new atheists' who write about Christianity, do not sufficiently engage with theology or the best thinking of Christian theologians. John F. Haught for example describes the new atheism as 'theologically unchallenging. Its engagement with theology lies at about the same level of reflection on faith that one can find in contemporary creationist and fundamentalist literature'. This may be true in some instances, but as a response to critiques of the Christian religion it is wearing a bit thin. Haught is particularly concerned with the writings of Dawkins, Harris and Hitchens, though he does mention others. But to say as he does, that 'none of (the new atheists) exhibits scholarly expertise in the field of religious studies', or that they have 'methodically avoided theologians and biblical scholars as irrelevant to the kind of instruction their books are intended to provide', is patently false. As a 'new' atheist myself, I certainly want to engage with serious theological thinking and writing, much of it already part of my essential study during the years of my Christian ministry.

As I survey the literature both for and against religious faith and Christianity in particular, I could lay the same charge of insufficient engagement at Haught's feet. It frustrates me that Christian writers rallying in response to this renewed questioning of their faith, seldom interact with the best atheist/humanist authors. The bibliographies of their defences of the Faith consistently either ignore or are unaware of some of the most challenging publications available today. It may be that they are so busy fighting a rearguard action that they haven't had time yet to address the extent and depth of the critique of religious faith. And since they need to write for a general or popular Christian market, they probably want to avoid the more sophisticated sources of criticism. After all, any studied analysis of the best in atheist writing today might reveal too much and have the opposite effect on believers seeking reassurance for their faith.

A few years ago I retired from the ministry of the Christian Church. Prior to that I had long entertained serious doubts about some of the very doctrines I had preached, explained and defended over a number of years. Today I no longer struggle with those doubts, or with what Paul Kurtz called 'The Transcendental Temptation.' Over the last few years I have had my new worldview greatly encouraged and affirmed by the reading of so many titles by secular humanist and atheist authors. Ironically, a number of those books have been authored by individuals who were once people of faith, several of them ex-ministers like myself. There seems to be a virtual avalanche of books and articles promoting reason and humanism and they are having a real impact on society. Religion in general and Christianity in particular, are increasingly on the defensive, barely comprehending the new wave of thinking and acting that is winning hearts and minds and gaining substantial inroads into the ranks of the believers—particularly young believers.

No one should question the immense benefits Western Civilisation has derived from the Christian religion. They hardly need defending. It is easy to focus on its intolerance, persecutions, violence and horrors and to find the obvious faults with its sacred Scripture. Nevertheless, millions of lives have been enriched, inspired and fortified by the faith of Christianity. Despite historic and present scandals, Christian character, morals and actions are more often praiseworthy, commendable and worth imitating. While I try to be sensitive to what I consider the illusions that give Christians comfort and hope, I am not willing to acquiesce or remain silent in the presence of 'god-talk' which constantly challenges me and others to consider the claim of Christianity that I am 'lost' and in need of 'saving.' That is the claim the following chapters seek to demolish.

The 'Good News'?

*We must discard the doctrine of the Atonement,
because it is absurd and immoral.
We are not accountable for the sins of 'Adam'
and the virtues of Christ cannot be
transferred to us.*

Robert G. Ingersoll (1833-1899

Fundamental to Christian faith is the claim expressed in the Gospel of John, chapter 11, verses 25-26: 'Jesus said to her, 'I am the resurrection and the life. Those who believe in me, even though they die, will live, and everyone who lives and believes in me will never die. Do you believe this?' (New Revised Standard Version, NRSV). Jesus allegedly said this at the tomb of his friend Lazarus. Sometime later in this same gospel, Jesus is reported to have said to his confused disciples: 'I am the way, and the truth, and the life. No one comes to the Father except through me' (14:6). In the New Testament book of Acts, the apostle Peter appearing before the Jewish council in Jerusalem boldly declares: 'There is salvation in no one else, for there is no other name under heaven given among mortals by which we must be saved.'

And then there are the words of Christianity's greatest champion and promoter, Paul the Apostle, writing to his fellow Christians in ancient

Corinth about death, hope and the coming resurrection of the dead: 'If Christ has not been raised, your faith is futile and you are still in your sins. Then those also who have died in Christ have perished ... But in fact Christ has been raised from the dead, the first fruits of those who have died. For since death came through a human being, the resurrection of the dead has also come through a human being; for as all die in Adam, so all will be made alive in Christ' (First Corinthians 15:17-22).

Now on any reading of such Christian texts, it is clear to see that Christianity is not simply about following the *teachings* of Christ. If that were the case, then it would be difficult to see why most people would not choose instead to live by the teachings of the Jewish prophets, Epicureanism, the Stoics or those of the Buddha. But Christianity is not about following the teachings of Jesus—most of which are largely Jewish and hardly original. Christianity is about following *Jesus,* believing in *him.* The reason is obvious from the texts just quoted. Jesus *himself* is the way to God, to heaven, to salvation. There is no other way or religion that will do that for you. In other words, he is the saviour that everyone needs—everyone without exception—Jews, Muslims, Hindus, Buddhists, atheists, even 'liberal' Christians! It is what Jesus *did* that saves us, not anything he taught. And what he did was what he was purportedly born to do, and that is, die for our sins on the cross.

Christ's death is the means of salvation. Without it, without having a personal relationship with him, all of us are lost. By lost we mean, no resurrection to eternal life, no heaven, no divine reward, no bliss in an afterlife, only the kind of abandonment, misery, regret and utter, endless hopelessness that is expressed by the word 'Hell.' Now instinctively, many people recoil from this belief. It seems harsh, intolerant, exclusivist, even absurd. Their instincts are quite well justified because regardless of the endless tomes written in its defence, it *is* harsh, intolerant, exclusivist and absurd. I might add, that it is also demeaning of the God Christians claim they worship. After all, if there is a god, it hardly seems likely that *this* version of salvation should be regarded as somehow truer or superior to that of Jews, Hindus, Buddhists, even Muslims. Only in the Christian religion is salvation dependent on the founder and only in the Christian religion is the means of salvation so extraordinarily bizarre. *How* bizarre and even incoherent (lacking logical connection; inarticulate; loose, disjoined), is what this book seeks to demonstrate. The Cross of Christ which is the most profound symbol of Christian faith, the supreme expression of God's love, the glory of Christianity is, in reality, its greatest anomaly or abnormality.

Of course Christians will say that the saving death of Christ is a profound mystery that cannot fully be understood, so mysterious in fact that the Christian Church historically, has never come up with a single, universally-accepted theory or explanation for how it actually works. Most devout Christians would say they don't know *how* it works, only *that* it does. I take serious issue with the *that*. The crucifixion and death of Christ is not, as Christians assert, the central blessed 'mystery' of the Christian faith. On the contrary, it makes *no* sense. It is, in effect, nonsense.

A statement penned by Franz Rosenzweig in his 1916 wartime correspondence with the Christian, Eugen Rosenstock-Huessy serves as an assessment of the Christian teaching. In that correspondence he said that 'all these realistic arguments (for Christianity) are only fashionable cloaks to hide the single true metaphysical ground: that we (Jews) will not make common cause with the *world-conquering fiction* of Christian dogma'[1]. Christianity's central, most significant doctrine, the thing upon which the whole religious edifice rests, is the doctrine of the atoning death of Christ on the cross. An examination of that teaching readily exposes it weakness and vulnerability, the very weakness that leads to the charge of its being 'absurd and immoral', 'repugnant to justice and mercy', 'unethical and unbelievable.' If the scripture texts which I cited earlier are not to be taken seriously, then Christianity is a mirage, a colossal piece of wishful thinking, not only a malignant mutation of Judaism, but an offence to common sense and a wilful rejection of the more plausible schemes of salvation expressed by other World religions.

That great enigma of first-century Judaism, Saul of Tarsus or Paul the Apostle, scorned the kind of wisdom and discernment expressed by the humanist philosophers of Athens. Not for him, the rational thinking that mocked Christian preaching about the cross and resurrection. 'For the message about the cross is foolishness to those who are perishing, but to us who are being saved it is the power of God ... Has not God made foolish the wisdom of the world? For since, in the wisdom of God, the world did not know God through wisdom (read, rational thought, reflection, studied investigation etc.,) God decided, through the foolishness of our proclamation, to save those who believe.' Paul then dismisses two groups of humanity, the religious and the philosophic. 'For Jews demand signs and Greeks desire wisdom, but we proclaim Christ crucified, a stumbling block to Jews and foolishness to Gentiles'. (1 Corinthians 1:18-25). My intention in the chapters which follow is, among other things, to side with the Gentiles (Greeks/humanists), to show why 'Christ crucified' really is a stumbling block and foolishness for any earnest, open-minded person not seduced by plausible-sounding god-talk.

The English word 'gospel' (from the Anglo-Saxon *god-spell*, i.e. God-story) is the usual New Testament translation of the Greek word *euangelion*. The gospel is supposed to be the joyous ('good news' or) proclamation of God's redemptive activity in Christ Jesus on behalf of man enslaved in sin' (*Evangelical Dictionary of Theology*, Walter A. Elwell, Editor). I am part of a growing and not so silent minority of secular humanists and atheists who have no reason to believe that the 'gospel' *is* God's story. Even if there were a God, it is not likely that he would come up with a scheme for the salvation of the human race as bizarre and incomprehensible as that which Christianity proclaims. Christianity, like all other religions is a tribute to the creative, sometimes noble religious imagination of the human species, but it is not attributable to any god, at least not any god who might inhabit the kind of cosmos that science has today made us aware of.

In asserting that the Gospel or 'Good News' isn't really good news, I often think about Christianity's 'parent-religion', Judaism. My first stirrings of doubt and serious questioning of Christianity began with an exposure to Judaism and ended with the conclusion that Christianity is no improvement on Judaism, and certainly not a replacement for it, or fulfillment of it. Instead, Christianity is a darker mutation of Judaism, particularly in its view of human nature, sin, forgiveness and salvation. I am convinced that if more people were acquainted with the Jewish belief about sin and salvation, they would be far less inclined to take the Christian view for granted. Judaism by its very nature, constitutes a serious critique of the Christian worldview and serves as a valuable resource in exposing the absurdity and harshness of the Christian view. The Christian story which has been promoted to the present day is fatally flawed, not only because it is essentially irrational and bizarre, but because those who knew it best in the beginning—the Jews of Judaea—rejected it.

Of course as an atheist, I do not mean to suggest that Judaism presents us with any more evidence for the existence of God or the reality of faith, but I do want to show that the Christianity which believes it has superseded or supplanted Judaism is, in fact, as I have already said, a serious aberration of the religion it broke away from. The religious imagination has not been well served by the Christian version of salvation. Another way of putting this is to say that Christianity and the role of Christ as saviour was never *necessary* or needful, but rather a betrayal of the finer, more humanistic elements of Judaism. And if the on-going studies on the 'Jewishness' of Jesus are telling us anything, it is that Jesus himself would have agreed with this assessment.

Two Testaments
Two Different Bibles

'Judaism and Christianity are completely different religions, not different versions of one religion (that of the 'Old Testament' or 'the written Torah'). The two faiths stand for different people talking about different things to different people.'
- Jacob Neusner

Because Christianity—originally a Jewish sect—has become overwhelmingly, the dominant world religion casting a giant shadow over tiny Judaism, the propaganda for salvation, sin, forgiveness and God's love has been almost exclusively a *Christian* story. To understand why a saviour is unnecessary and why Christianity was not inevitable, we have to remember that the original Biblical story is really about God the Father, for *he* is the one who forgives. *Why* he forgives, *how* he forgives, is the real 'Gospel' we might say. At least within a religious context, one I no longer operate within, Judaism knew the answer all along. As I said, my first crisis of faith years ago was born out of that realisation. I initially suppressed that realisation because it threatened to abolish Christ.

If what three-quarters of what we call the Bible, i.e. the Hebrew Scriptures, consistently and clearly tells us about the forgiveness of God is true, then the other quarter (the New Testament) is in serious error. The 'New' Testament may be *new*, but it is not an outgrowth of the so-called 'Old' Testament. There is no 'new' covenant, only a *new religion*, Christianity. As Jacob Neusner has written: 'Judaism and Christianity are completely different religions, not different versions of one religion (that of the 'Old Testament' or 'the written Torah'). The two faiths stand for different people talking about different things to different people.'[1] In that sense I am not denying Jesus, because I believe that he belongs to the old tradition, not the new one.

Anyone who still wants to believe in God and reads the Bible, must see that he is faced with this choice. Either God can choose to show mercy and forgive us because we repent (Judaism), or he forgives us, but only *after* he has had satisfaction for the offences committed against him (Christianity). And by satisfaction we mean it in the Christian sense, that a penalty must be paid, a punishment must be endured *before* God can forgive. Surely though, plain common sense, tells us that forgiveness can't really be forgiveness if it is based on punishment, on blood atonement. This is why the choice is so stark and so poignant, because it is a choice between *two kinds of God*. Years ago I came to the conclusion that the God of the 'Old' Testament, the Jewish God, Jesus's God, made more sense.

The supreme irony is that, despite the popular misconception, it is the God of the *Old* Testament or Covenant who, in reality, seems more compassionate, more gracious, more loving and more forgiving, than the so-called New Testament God of love and grace. The Old Testament God forgives a penitent King David in Psalm 51—read it and see—but seems unable to do the same for anyone in the New Testament. In this added testament, it is the Cross of Christ and the teachings of St. Paul which reveal a God who is unspeakably harsh, unnecessarily judicial and terrifyingly intolerant of human imperfection.

Judaism's 'Good news' is that God freely forgives anyone who says he or she is truly sorry for having done wrong. The Jewish God judges us by our behaviour and conduct towards others, not by our belief in particular dogmas. It is because Judaism takes that approach that it is not an *exclusive* religion in the way that Christianity is. In Jewish eyes, the good people of any faith will find a place in heaven. You don't have to be Jewish to be 'saved.' But because Christianity has this God who cannot forgive you unless you believe specific things about a saviour, blood atonement and the necessity of a human sacrifice, it must insist that only through the Christian saviour can *anyone* be saved.

In 1939 the Christian writer Rev. Dr. A. Lukyn Williams, member of Jesus College, Cambridge, wrote these words in his book *The Doctrines of Modern Judaism Considered*: 'The Christian holds that his sin must be met in some way, and that mere forgiveness by God is not sufficient in itself. Mere forgiveness of sin seems to be immoral!'[2] Those words express what I believe, is the crucial difference between Judaism and Christianity. An historic, complex and much debated Christian theology of atonement has sought to explain and justify those words—'mere forgiveness by God is not sufficient in itself.'

The defence of such an astonishing assertion is necessary for Christianity to maintain its historic claim as the replacement for God's covenant with the people of Israel. For if the forgiveness of God can be shown to be sufficient, as the Old Testament amply affirms, then there can be no need for an atonement based on the vicarious suffering and death of a saviour. Though Christian apologists today may not be so willing to use a phrase like *mere* forgiveness, for fear it may seem to denigrate what God actually does, the sense of what they continue to teach about salvation and the cross of Jesus, is that they still believe what Lukyn Williams was saying. In other words, a measure of denigration remains.

Of course as an atheist, I do not believe that any kind of divine forgiveness is *necessary* for humankind, since there is no divine being to offer it, but I can't make an effective critique of the Christian view of salvation without putting in a good word, so to speak, for Judaism. Judaism simply does not warrant some of the same criticisms of God levelled by numerous authors against Christianity.

The Christian apologist C.S. Lewis, for all his gifts as a great communicator, still maintained the historic Christian negative assessment of human nature which is largely absent from Judaism. Christianity seems to totally ignore the experience of millions in every age who have lived quiet, simple, decent lives and been good neighbours and friends. It ignores the far more positive view of human nature that has always been expressed by Judaism. The whole intent of such a negative appraisal of human nature is to paint the bleakest possible picture of the human moral dilemma. Only by doing that can Christianity then introduce a solution or response that is also extreme and negative. They call it the 'Gospel' the good news because it relieves the minds of those troubled by the previous bad news. 'The death and resurrection of Christ' Lewis insists, 'is the only way to redeem humanity's sins.' Any student of world religions would take issue with that conclusion. No other major world religion suggests such a radical solution to human sin—certainly not Judaism, the religion of Jesus.

God 'became a man' in Christ, Lewis says, so that mankind could be 'amalgamated with God's nature' and make full atonement possible. Lewis offers several analogies to explain this strange concept. He suggests that Jesus was 'paying the penalty' for a crime, 'paying a debt,' or helping humanity out of an impossibly desperate situation. As if suspecting how bizarre the Christian view of atonement and salvation must sound to any rational person, Lewis admits that redemption is so incomprehensible that it cannot be fully appreciated, and he attempts to explain that *how* God atones for sin is not nearly as important as the fact that he does. I think this is a telling admission.

Some time in 1943, Lewis adopted the words *Mere Christianity* for his own apologetic purpose. In his Introduction to *St. Athanasius, On the Incarnation*, translated from the Greek by his friend Sister Penelope Lawson, CSMV, Lewis wrote: 'The only safety against the theological errors in recently published books,' wrote Lewis, 'is to have a standard of plain, central Christianity ('mere Christianity' as Baxter called it) which puts the controversies of the moment in their proper perspective.'[3]

Those 'controversies of the moment', now very old, but no less troublesome, are truly the Achilles heel of Christianity. Thousands of times every day of the week and every week of the year, Christians are sharing the 'good news' of the Gospel with friends and neighbours. They are telling them in varying degrees of sensitivity and competency, that everyone is lost in sin and needs the forgiveness and spirit of Christ in order to be put right with God and made worthy of ultimate entry into eternal life—Heaven. If, as even Christian surveys and studies show, hundreds of thousands are deserting the Church every year, part of the reason surely, is that this so-called 'good news' really does sound 'as hard as nails' (Lewis's words) and much as they have tried to understand it and believe it, they have concluded that it is simply nonsense. Among the questions we might ask about this peculiar view of salvation are these:

1. The Christian idea of salvation only through Jesus Christ means that the many who have not heard of Jesus or had the opportunity to accept the 'Good News' about him, are automatically considered lost, or if not lost, provided for in some retroactive, mystical way. The salvation of God in Judaism—and *most* other world religions—is wider and more profound than the narrower way that is offered only through faith in Jesus Christ. These other faiths see the earnest seeker after God in whatever World Faith, to have access to God, his forgiveness, grace and redemption. Judaism does not see itself as the exclusive way to God.

2. Why is God unable to forgive us apart from the vicarious atonement of Jesus?

3. Why, according to the Christian doctrine of Original Sin, is the whole human race held accountable for Adam's sin? Why are we *all* condemned because of what *he* did? Why does the Jewish part of the Bible, which includes the Book of Deuteronomy, clearly state that, 'Parents shall not be put to death for their children, *nor shall children be put to death for their parents* (emphasis mine); only for their own crimes may persons be put to death.' (24:16). The clearest rebuttal to the Christian dogma of Original sin is found in Ezekiel chapter 18: 1-24. It contains phrases such as, 'He shall not die for his father's iniquity ... Yet you say, 'Why should not the son suffer for the iniquity of his father'? The person who sins shall die. A child shall not suffer for the iniquity of a parent ... the righteousness of the righteous shall be his own, and the wickedness of the wicked shall be his own.' No wonder Jews think the Christians have a different God. Verse 25, could be cited to express the difference between Judaism and Christianity succinctly: 'Hear now, O house of Israel: is my way unfair? Is it not your ways that are unfair?'

4. Why is 'mere forgiveness' not enough?

5. *Who* is it that died for us on the cross? If it was the Son and not the Father, as orthodox Christian teaching asserts, how can the doctrine of ONE God—even in 'three persons'—be maintained?

6. How can the God-forsakenness which Jesus experienced on the cross—'My God, my God, why have you forsaken me!?'—be adequately explained if he *is* God? How can God forsake God?

7. Why does God have to sacrifice *himself*—or his Son—in order to forgive us, when the 'Old' Testament is filled with examples of God forgiving people out of sheer mercy, love and grace? What has changed?

8. How can Psalm 51, the great psalm of repentance, be explained other than in a Jewish sense where God forgives the truly repentant simply because they repent? Why did King David not need some future vicarious atonement to cover or put away his sin? Why does he say in verse 16 that the Lord 'does not delight in sacrifice, or I would bring it'? Why does David say that the real sacrifices for sin 'are a broken spirit and a contrite heart', which is the essential message of the prophets? Again, what changed with the advent of the Christian religion?

9. Why is the God of the 'Old' Testament, seemingly more gracious and forgiving, willing to 'blot out transgressions' because he chooses to do so, than the God of the New Testament who requires a blood atonement or human vicarious sacrifice in order to do so?

10. Why do Christians, referring to the verse in Leviticus about there being no possibility of atonement without the shedding of blood, not see that they take the verse out of context; that atonement in the 'Old' Testament is *not* always dependent on a blood offering; that other than blood offerings or sacrifices were acceptable to God?

11. Does not the 'Old' Testament make it clear that vicarious blood atonement was NOT ever offered for deliberate or intentional sins, but only for *un*intentional sins? (Numbers 15:27-31).

12. How can Christians escape the fact that repentance in the 'Old' Testament results in forgiveness, that people do not need a mediator or vicarious sacrifice in order to put themselves right with God?

13. Why is it that the Jewish people in the dispersion, in Babylon, Egypt and elsewhere, were able to maintain a relationship with God, including forgiveness of their sins, without access to a temple, priesthood or sacrifices? Is it really sufficient to say, as some Christians do, that God was merely temporarily covering their sins, until full satisfaction could be made for them in the future death of Jesus? Doesn't that undermine

or unjustifiably qualify the love and mercy of God who, it is claimed, did forgive people in the past?

14. Why has the Christian Church never been able to produce a theory of the Atonement that has won universal support? Why does the Atonement as Christians understand it, remain a profound mystery? Ask your Christian friend to explain it to you and see if it makes any sense.

15. The 'Penal' or 'substitutionary' view of the Atonement, a view promoted by the Evangelical and particularly by those of the Reformed (Calvinist branch of Protestantism) faith, suggests things about God and man which we should find strange and abhorrent. For example, if Jesus took our place on the cross, if he is literally our substitute, does that mean that God really thinks of *us* as deserving of torture and crucifixion or death? Is all human sin equally reprehensible and deserving of so severe a punishment? And if the Jewish people find this idea strange and abhorrent, who can blame atheists for having that same reaction?

16. If the only righteousness God will accept is *perfect* righteousness, i.e. no human being can be good enough to satisfy God's requirements; we all 'fall short' and are in need of saving grace—the kind Jesus exhibited—why are there so many verses in the 'Old' Testament that assure us that God does *not* expect perfection of us; that he has mercy on us because he knows we are imperfect and remembers that we are dust?

When I conducted communion services in my last parish church, I always read from Psalm 103. It was a subversive exercise because I was already convinced that the Christian view of atonement was seriously flawed. Here we were handling the elements of bread and grape juice which reminded us of Christ's necessary and atoning sacrifice and at the same time hearing words of Scripture strongly suggesting that such a sacrifice wasn't necessary! I always used to wonder if the 'penny dropped' for anyone in the congregation. 'He does not deal with us according to our sins, nor repay us according to our iniquities ... as far as the east is from the west, so far he removes our transgression from us. As a father has compassion for his children, so the Lord has compassion for those who fear him.' And then follows the crucially telling verse, 'For he knows how we were made; he remembers that we are dust' (10-14). No expectation of perfection there. No need for a Saviour, just the sincere repentance of weak, flawed, imperfect people.

If God's standard of righteousness is perfection, how could he ever have expected us to please him? Where in all the scriptures does it say we need to live perfect lives in order to be acceptable to God? Isn't this alleged lack of perfection the reason why Christians say we need a 'perfect' substitute in order to be saved? Given that the perfect substitute is supposed to be God himself in the person of Jesus, is it fair of God to demand perfection of us? Judaism says no, Christianity says yes.

16. If God cannot forgive us without the vicarious punishment or atoning sacrifice of Jesus, is that really forgiveness? If *we* refused to forgive people unless they were also punished, or after they were first punished, would we really be forgiving them? And even if the punishment is vicarious, as Christians assert, isn't this still less than forgiveness, less than sheer grace?

As an ordained Christian minister I always approached the Easter season with considerable preparation and sensitivity. Knowing that my congregations had heard the Easter story told many times in their lives, I tried to make my Easter messages more informative, compelling and emotional. Easter was always a journey from Palm Sunday to the Resurrection morning, a liturgical journey full of symbolism, historical and cultural context, realism and emotion as we sought to identify with the experiences of our saviour Jesus.

In my first years of ministry, my sermons were more 'Reformed', filled with the stark realities of this harsh doctrine of Atonement. Christ stood between us and the wrath of God for our sins. Only his death was capable of absorbing that wrath and making it possible for grace to trump justice. We should have received what we *deserved*—condemnation, judgment and eternal death, but the Cross brought us forgiveness and peace with God. So long as we accepted that we were lost sinners deserving of God's terrible judgment and that by accepting Christ's death in place of our own, then we were 'saved'. Easter was always a profound and sobering experience.

Later in my ministry I became more liberal in my views. I was troubled by questions of election. Has God really chosen only *some* for salvation and decided not to extend saving grace to others as John Calvin taught? Did Christ really die on the cross only for the elect (limited atonement)? What about the millions who never heard of Christ, or if they had, remained true to their own religions? My more liberal views helped me to cope with such tensions and I adopted a more 'catholic' view of salvation. In the end however, liberalism doesn't really work. If you believe that Christ died merely as a moral example to inspire us or that his submissive death demonstrated the love and compassion of God, because the idea of him being punished in our stead seemed too crude, too demeaning of God, then you were still left wondering *why* he had to die on the Cross at all. Liberalism tends to shift the emphasis back to the example and teachings of Jesus, whereas Christianity is essentially a message about who Jesus was and is—'God with us—Emanuel'.

Liberal Christianity ends up drifting a long way from the historic Christian faith and robbing the religion of its founder's role as saviour. If you are Roman Catholic for example, what is the most commonly-observed sacred rite or sacrament? It is the Eucharist or the Mass, a remembrance of Christ's body and blood given for us. He literally died for us and not just as an example, for many ordinary human beings have done that. No, his death was an 'atonement'. It actually achieved something. Billions of Christians for two millennia have believed that and, more astonishingly, have believed that at the Mass they are actually eating the flesh and drinking the blood of God the Son. It's hard to have a liberal view of the Mass or Eucharist.

Protestants will argue that they don't believe in the miracle of transubstantiation and that the bread and wine (or grape juice) they partake of, are merely symbols of Christ's life given for us. Nevertheless, Protestants still believe in the miracle of the atonement, that this particular death somehow mystically achieves forgiveness and reconciliation with God. *How* it does this remains a profound mystery, which is always better than thinking it is titanic nonsense. It is the sequel to the Cross, namely the resurrection on Easter Sunday morning that is offered as the final 'proof' that it did work. But that has to be taken on faith too.

Increasingly I found that passionate though my Easter sermons were, I myself remained somewhat unconvinced. Most of the time I kept that to myself, but in my last few years in ministry was able to share it with members of my congregation in some Bible studies. It was always a surprise to see how some in the studies responded positively to negative critiques of traditional Christian views. When we studied World Religions it was not unusual for some members of my congregation to conclude that Judaism had a better, fairer, more compassionate view of salvation and a healthier grasp of human nature and the limitations of human character. It would take some years before I disavowed any belief in God as well as Christ. I now wonder why I spent so much time and energy struggling with the theological absurdities that are the inevitable consequences of religions produced by human imagination.

Eugene Borowitz, a Jewish theologian, speaks for Judaism generally when he states that: 'We consider unduly harsh the concept of a God who does not accept each person's repentance. That, instead, God responds to an innocent person's suffering—Jesus' crucifixion and death—as atoning compensation for the guilty seems to us utterly unethical and unbelievable.'[4] Did you get that last phrase—'utterly unethical and unbelievable.'

The next time some well-meaning Christian is trying to persuade you that you are lost and in need of saving by Christ, tell him that you find his Christian Gospel utterly unethical and unbelievable. Tell him that it is not only atheists who respond like that to Christianity, but Jews. Judaism is the soil out of which Christianity grew. It gave Christianity its Jesus, its first converts, its scriptures with all their stories, prophets and wisdom. Most significantly, it gave Christians their God, the God of 'Abraham, Isaac and Jacob.' Tell them that this religion, so intimately related to their own, considers their story about Christ and his cross 'unethical and unbelievable.' Be bold, don't be afraid to give a little offence. It might stir up some serious thinking on their part. And after all, Christianity has had a pretty fair go in Western Civilization for the past eighteen centuries or so. Shouldn't Christians be aware that a religion which has been around a thousand years longer than their own, is not impressed with their Christian Gospel?

The 'Fall' and Human 'Lostness'

'The very thought that God would require the violent death of Jesus himself as a sin offering before forgiveness could be granted would have been repulsive to the mind of Jesus, as it is to our minds today'
- Rev. Dr. Samuel Angus,
Professor of New Testament and Historical Theology,
St. Andrew's College, University of Sydney, 1934.

Almost everyone, Christian and non-Christian, knows that Jesus Christ died on a cross two thousand years ago. We know *why* he died. In the religious and political context of first-century Judaea, a province of the Roman Empire, anyone suspected of being Israel's long-awaited Messiah or deliverer could become the focus of rebellion against Rome. Whether or not Jesus intended to be a martyr or simply got caught up in events beyond his control resulting in his execution, his death or execution is not disputed. What is disputed is what that death *meant*. Was it inevitable? Was it necessary? Was it beneficial in any way? Christians believe that it *was* inevitable, it *was* necessary and it *was* beneficial. Consider one of the most famous verses in the New Testament—John 3:16, 'For God so loved the world that he gave his only Son, so that everyone who believes in him may not perish but may have eternal life.' A few verses later the issue is further clarified. 'Those who believe in him are not condemned; but those who do not believe are condemned already.' Now what exactly is this verse saying?

First of all, everyone is 'lost'—spiritually. Everyone is a 'sinner' deserving of God's condemnation and judgment. Everyone is destined for an eternal separation from God, a punishment beyond imagination. Hell is the word used most frequently to describe it. One prominent Evangelical theologian who expresses this confronting teaching is I. Howard Marshall. He used to be one of my favourite Bible commentators.

> A traditional and very simple understanding of what happens in the death of Jesus Christ would be as follows. First, all humankind is condemned to eternal death as the penalty imposed by God for human sin. No matter how much or how little we may have sinned, there is a fixed penalty for all sinners, namely eternal death, of which physical death is both a part and a symbol. Second, the death of Jesus on the cross was not merely a physical death but also the eternal death due to sinners.[1]

That's the *bad* news. Most people hearing this are usually bewildered. They didn't realise that they were lost, nor were they aware that they were already 'condemned' by God. The destiny of every living person is to 'perish', not just physically at the end of their mortal life, but for all eternity after their death. Marshall states this belief so matter-of-factly, so clinically, that after a second's reflection, it almost takes your breath away. Just think of two of his phrases—'all humankind is condemned to eternal death.' Eternal death! And 'no matter how much or how little we may have sinned', the penalty is still 'eternal death.'

Now most people are willing to admit that they aren't perfect, that they have some serious weaknesses or addictions and that they often fall short of their own best intentions. But they are also aware that most of the time they lead pretty decent lives, love their families, do an honest day's work, enjoy sharing the good things of life with others, feel distressed by the suffering and exploitation of others, help their neighbours when they can, and generally try to be good people. There are exceptions of course, but happily we are talking about *most* people. They may not feel particularly religious, but that does not prevent them from living ethically or morally and doing what they think is right. The idea that they are 'lost' in God's eyes sounds strange because they are not particularly aware that God, if he does exist—and most are willing to believe that he might—concerns himself with their individual lives or behaviour. In fact in rare moments of reflection, they agree that 'something' must be responsible for all that exists, but when it comes to a personal God, such a being appears to be hidden or invisible, silent and inert. He doesn't do anything or make himself obvious.

They are sure that if such a personal god did exist and made himself more obvious, that they would feel obliged to believe in him. But then given the great variety of religions in the world with all their competing views of God, they conclude that it is really very difficult to decide which one is telling the truth. But now Christianity comes to such people and tells them that before they can hear the *good* news—the 'Gospel' of salvation, they have to understand the *bad* news and that is that they deserve eternal death. When I think of all the clever and persuasive ways I tried to communicate this stark, disturbing truth in so many sermons and evangelistic situations, I am frankly ashamed that I could ever have entertained such convictions.

Living as they do in a multi-cultural society like Australia or the United States or the United Kingdom, why should it be Christ particularly that they should believe in in order not to perish and have eternal life? Most know about other World religions but probably not enough to decide whether a billion Hindus or more than a billion Muslims might have the key to eternal life. And then there are about half a billion Buddhists who seem to be very decent, peaceful, compassionate, balanced people, so much so that they suspect this Buddha character must have been a pretty special human being—perhaps at least as special as Christ. Why shouldn't they believe in *him* in order not to perish and have eternal life? They might even know enough about Buddhism to know that Buddhists don't believe in God or gods, that Buddha himself was not a saviour, but someone who taught us that we must all find our own way to 'enlightenment.' Is Buddha also lost? What about the Dalai Lama? He seems like a good man and he certainly knows about Jesus Christ, because he has friends like Archbishop Desmond Tutu. But the Dalai Lama doesn't *believe in* Jesus, at least not as a saviour or God-incarnate.

Mahatma Ghandi was a devout Hindu. Most people religious or not, think of him as a very good man. He too knew all about Jesus and the New Testament, but he didn't *believe in* Jesus either—not in the way that Christians insist that we must. Is Gandhi lost too? Numerous Christian articles have been written about the 'Gandhi-dilemma' with titles like 'Is Gandhi in Heaven?' Liberal-minded Christians go through all kinds of theological gymnastics to suggest that there must be a place in God's mercy and heaven for people like Gandhi, even though the clear teaching of the New Testament doesn't really allow for such wishful thinking.

More conservative or evangelical Christians feel awkward and defensive when asked the question, but generally and gently insist that, as the Bible says, 'There is salvation in no one else, for there is no other name under heaven given among mortals by which we must be saved' (Acts 4:12). The average citizen hearing that the Dalai Lama and Gandhi aren't good enough for heaven may feel somewhat worried. More likely they will conclude that this is simply ridiculous. This 'lostness' thing has been carried too far. How did we get 'lost' anyway?

The great Christian myth—borrowed from the Jewish part of the Bible (Genesis) and given a different interpretation—is that the first human being was Adam. The second was Eve. Placed in the garden of Eden they broke a promise not to eat of the fruit of 'the tree of the knowledge of good and evil', because 'in the day that you eat of it you shall die' (Genesis 2:17).

The Devil in the form of a snake and with the voice of a human being, tempted Eve to break her promise to God. She ate the forbidden fruit, convinced Adam to do the same and that had cosmic consequences. God was very angry and condemned them both. She was doomed to have increased pains in childbirth and, as the female of the human species, to be dominated by men. Life was to get very much harder, work would become arduous and nature itself would be changed.

Formed out of the dust they were informed by God that 'to dust you shall return.' They were then expelled from Paradise and thrust out into a new, cruel, inhospitable world. I say cruel and inhospitable because Christianity teaches that before the 'Fall' the whole Earth was a paradise with no death or suffering. After the 'Fall' death and suffering entered the world. Not only that, but some kind of genetic mutation occurred in the human offspring of Adam and Eve so that all the billions of people descended from them, inherited this 'original sin' and became worthy of God's condemnation and judgment and destined for eternal death. This is the Christian doctrine of the 'Fall'.

Even people who aren't particularly religious or don't attend church services have probably at some time or another, attended a church service to witness a friend's baby being baptized.' In Catholic, Anglican and orthodox churches, the baptism of infants is a holy 'sacrament'. This means it is an infusion of God's miraculous 'grace' which dilutes the stain of original sin with which the child was born, providing it with an antidote that makes it capable of experiencing God's favour and ultimately being 'saved.' Listen carefully next time you attend such a service and take note of the words the priest or minister says. There is no doubt that this sacred rite is tied to original sin and the hope of salvation. 'The one who believes and is baptized will be saved; but the one who does not believe will be condemned.' Baptism washes away sin and gives us a fresh start. It does not guarantee final salvation, but it does mean that we are no longer 'lost' and destined to 'perish'.

To the average person this might seem like an over-reaction on God's part. After all, how could Adam and Eve be condemned for doing the *wrong* thing by eating the fruit if they did not have the 'knowledge of good and evil' before they ate it? Most think of the story as a fairy-tale, a moral fable meant to communicate something serious or profound, but conservative, evangelical Christians believe the story must be taken literally. There was a garden somewhere, a naked couple did inhabit it, enjoying perfect bliss. There were no weeds or thorns and a snake was capable of talking—even perhaps of walking, because God cursed the snake (no wonder most of us don't like them!) and condemned it to crawl upon its belly and eat dust.

Most Jews don't take this story literally, but Christians are almost obliged to. If Christians don't take it literally then they have a massive problem that really is the Achilles Heel of Christianity. Once you grasp the nature of this problem, you see that the whole Christian edifice built on the idea of salvation through Christ's death on a cross is simply preposterous. Why is there a problem? Because of the apostle Paul who bequeathed to Christianity a whole set of theological problems. We find the answer in his First letter to the Corinthians, chapter 15, verses 21 and 22.

In Paul's thinking the persons of Adam and Christ are inextricably linked. 'For since death came through a human being, the resurrection of the dead has also come through a human being; for as all die in Adam, so all will be made alive in Christ.' It is as if Adam fatally infected the entire human species with a deadly virus that will eventually kill them. Theologians call this virus 'original sin'. Christ by contrast, provides the serum or antidote that can cure this virus and bring us back to health. Christ does this, not by anything he teaches us, but by his death on the cross. Again, it seems to serve no purpose to ask the theologians how that works.

The first thing that needs to be said about this strange view of the human condition is that it has been totally discredited by science—anthropology, biology, genetics. No one, except for young-Earth creationists—seriously doubts today that the human species is hundreds of thousands of years old; that it first appeared in Africa rather than the Garden of Eden, and that there never was a time in Eden, Shangri-la or anywhere else where death and decay were absent. The biological history of life on earth has been an unimaginably long process that has witnessed over hundreds of millions of years, the mass extinctions of whole species, predation and death. Human beings have a very long primate evolutionary history.

Long before Adam and Eve frolicked in Eden, when apparently there were no climate extremes, no natural disasters, nothing died or decayed, there had been at least seventeen severe ice ages over a 2.5 million year period, a period that coincides with the rise of *Homo Erectus* in Africa, the species which emerged just before our own. Our ancestors roamed the earth for several million years. Our particular species—*Homo sapiens,* appeared in Africa during a time of dramatic climate change about 200,000 years ago. There were other early 'humans' living at this time. By about 164,000 years ago modern humans were collecting and cooking shellfish and by 90,000 years ago they had begun making special fishing tools. Only within the last 12,000 years, have *Homo sapiens* made the transition to an agricultural mode of living. One of the groups which overlapped the period of our own species was the Neanderthals, our closest extinct human relative. Discovered in 1829, they lived in Europe and southwestern to central Asia 200,000 to 40,000 years ago.

I remember as a Christian minister when we were involved in debates about evolution (I was liberal on the issue, an 'evolutionary theist'), buying books about the Neanderthals and wondering how God regarded them. They posed a special problem because while we assumed any primate before our human species would not have had a 'soul', Neanderthals clearly 'made and used a diverse set of sophisticated tools, controlled fire, lived in shelters, made and wore clothing, were skilled hunters of large animals and also ate plant foods, and occasionally made symbolic or ornamental objects. There is evidence that Neanderthals deliberately buried their dead and occasionally even marked their graves with offerings, such as flowers. No other primates, and no earlier human species, had ever practiced this sophisticated and symbolic behavior.'

The DNA recovered from more than a dozen Neanderthal fossils from all over Europe has now shown that our two species did make contact, did inter-breed on a limited basis resulting in the fact that human beings today have between 1% and 4% Neanderthal DNA in their biological make-up. We share a common ancestor but *Homo Sapiens* are not descended from Neanderthals.[2] How, I wondered, did these close relatives fit into the divine scheme. Obviously they were here *before* Adam and they displayed a lot of human-like qualities. They lived in small groups, had families, nurtured their children, made hunting tools, suffered pain, experienced happiness, wore clothes and thought enough about the meaning of life to bury their dead with ceremony. Were they saved by the 'blood of Christ'? Did God love them too? The real story of human origins is so much grander, profound and verifiable than the myths of Genesis. Human beings as well as Neanderthals lived and *died* thousands if not hundreds of thousands of years before the 'Fall' depicted in Genesis.

Being a liberal Christian as I once was, I simply adopted the 'enlightened' view of many Christians and now of the Catholic Church officially, that Darwinian Evolution was God's means of creating life on earth. It is always very telling to see how the church constantly adapts itself to discoveries in the advancement of science. It's been doing that since Galileo's time as well as Darwin's. While it made me feel more comfortable with the religion-science relationship, it could not ultimately stave off the niggling suspicion that religion does not basically deal with reality.

How could I be an evolutionary-theist and still preach that 'As in Adam all die, so in Christ shall all be made alive'? Humans *didn't* all 'die' because of Adam's sin. Death and decay did not enter the world as a result of Adam's sin—it had already existed for hundreds of millions of years as part of the natural order. Such an assertion was simply an expression of the mind of a first-century, non-scientific man called Paul who knew nothing about human origins or the origins of the world and who claimed that he received his knowledge by 'revelation.' How can Christians who preach the Gospel to us, expect us to accept *their* 'solution' to our human dilemma of being 'lost' when they are fundamentally wrong about the *cause* requiring that solution? 1 Corinthians 15:21-22 is a statement of faith. It has no more credibility as a statement of the way things really are than any ancient Greek mythological account of the gods or creation.

I am still astonished to read Christian defences of the Faith which try to salvage the Faith in the confronting face of science. Dr. Denis Alexander, Director of the Faraday Institute for Science and Religion, St. Edmund's College, Cambridge, has written in his book *Creation or Evolution? Do We have to Choose?* , 'Evolutionary history is perfectly consistent with the creator God revealed in the Bible who has intentions and purposes for the world, including us. Holding to evolution as a biological theory should not affect one whit the Christian's belief in the uniqueness of humankind made in God's image, the Fall, the reality of sin and our need for redemption through the atoning work of Christ on the cross for our sins.'[3] Over years of deep reflection and anxious doubt I repeatedly had to conclude about this and many other defences that they just don't get it!

Numerous liberal Christian writers and scientists like Alexander, valiantly attempt to wed reality with fantasy and it just doesn't work. It is one of the reasons why several recent Evangelical studies have lamented the substantial losses in numbers of young people leaving the Church. John S. Dickerson in his *The Great Evangelical Recession* writes that '260,000 evangelical young people walk away from Christianity each year. Of that number 35% will find their way back, and 65% do not find their way back.

Why are they leaving? *They don't believe anymore.*' (emphasis mine). He continues, 'This is not a blip. This is a trend. And the trend is one of decline.'[4] Now from my reading of the literature there are a number of reasons why they don't believe anymore, but prominent among them is their exposure to a scientific world-view.

The facts speak for themselves. Towards the end of his book, Alexander considers all the possibilities of fitting Adam into a puzzle which seems to have no spaces for him and concludes, 'there are certainly no genetic data suggesting that all humankind originated from one family in the Near East about 6,000-8,000 years ago', despite the fact that that period is Alexander's best bet for the existence of Adam and Eve. He understands the questions that Genesis provokes, for example, 'what was the eternal destiny of all those who lived before Adam and Eve? The answer really is that we have no idea.' What else can he say? But rather than say nothing, he falls back on that old reassuring evangelical comfort blanket by reminding his readers that, 'we can be assured with Abraham: 'Will not the judge of all the earth do right?' (Genesis 18:25). Thankfully, he is suggesting, we are not called to judge the earth and we can leave that safely in the hands of the one who 'judges justly' (1 Peter 2:23).'[5] When all the evidence continues to mount against your faith position, rather than concede or question the credibility of your faith, leave it to God. He'll sort it out. It is a classic Christian evasion of the question.

Living as I do in Australia, I share a continent with the world's oldest living culture. The Australian Aborigines have inhabited this great south land for about 60,000 years. That didn't escape Alexander's attention either. He admits that the question of what *their* eternal destiny was, long before Moses received the Law on Sinai, is a troubling and worthwhile question. But again, instead of actually dealing with this problem, he tells his readers, 'Again, we really don't know and, again, 'Will not the judge of all the earth do right?'[6]. Christian leaders worrying why droves of young people are leaving the Church need look no further than this kind of explanation for faith.

Thirty years ago, I first discovered the writings of that eminent historian Barbara W. Tuchman. I employed her phrase on 'cognitive dissonance' for my own analyses of a number of situations and issues. That phrase appears in her book *The March of Folly*. 'When objective evidence disproves strongly held beliefs, what occurs, according to theorists of 'cognitive dissonance', is not rejection of the beliefs but rigidifying, accompanied by attempts to rationalise the disproof. The result is 'cognitive rigidity;' in lay language, the knots of folly draw tighter.'[7] She was talking about U.S. foreign policy in the Vietnam War, but the phrase has proved most apt in trying to understand a number of religious or faith positions. Every now and then, I interrupt my readings of humanist and historical texts to re-read a work of Christian apologetics. Each time I do, I see afresh, those 'knots of folly' being drawn tighter and wonder why I didn't draw the conclusions I did about religion even earlier. In his book on evolution, human origins and Adam, Alexander exhibits a classic case of both cognitive dissonance and cognitive rigidity.

Dr. Russell Blackford is an Australian academic, a lecturer at the University of Newcastle and editor-in-chief of *The Journal of Evolution and Technology*. He was once the vice-president of the Evangelical Union of the University of Newcastle, but is now an atheist. Author and/or editor of a number of books, including *50 Great Myths About Atheism*, he describes how his doubts led him to question the Christian worldview. As he struggled with the works of Christian theologians and philosophers whose works provided defences of the Faith, he came to the point where 'All the answers were *highly* implausible at best. And too much else converged to cast extreme doubt on the whole Christian worldview, rather than to provide compelling reasons in its support.'[8]

So many ex-Christians like Blackford are accused by those they leave behind of seeking reasons *not* to believe, or of taking too 'intellectual' an approach to what are essentially matters of 'faith.' In reality, they have almost always been fervent advocates of the Christian Faith and known it well enough to convince others in the past that they should believe it. With the onset of doubt, they have usually re-acquainted themselves with all the strongest, most sophisticated defences of the Faith, trying to persuade themselves that their doubts were not justified. But as Blackford concluded, all the arguments in favour of Christianity, became increasingly 'implausible.' What irritates them about their one-time brethren, is that those same people who can't understand how they could possibly deny their Faith, are themselves unwilling to study any of the real challenges to Christianity. I personally find that puzzling.

More troubling is the fact that they aren't usually interested in studying defences of the Faith either. They just prefer to accept it all on faith and not get too 'technical' about it. It has certainly been my experience that most Christians who have expressed bewilderment at my change of worldview, are not in the least concerned with studying the reasons *why* I made that change. I suppose there is a sense in which they are afraid of being exposed to knowledge or information that may trouble or disturb their settled convictions.

It is true that Christians are much more likely to read books that give them reasons to believe, but only if some pastor or Christian friend enthusiastically recommends that they do so. Another Christian apologist who *is* read by Christians is Norman L. Geisler, co-author with Frank Turek of *I Don't Have Enough Faith to Be an Atheist.* Geisler treats the issue of Adam and the Fall in the form of a dialogue between 'Christian' and 'Atheist.' Atheist asks, if the source of evil is man's free choice, why do babies die? Why do natural disasters occur? And Christian answers, 'The Bible traces it all back to the fall of man. No one is really innocent (including the babies!) because we all sinned in Adam (Romans 5:12) and as a consequence deserve death (Rom.6:23). Natural disasters and premature deaths are a direct result of the curse on creation because of the fall of humankind (Genesis 3, Romans 8). This fallen world will not be righted until Christ returns.'[9]. Any sane, fair-minded person reading that would have to think, well, he doesn't have enough faith to be an atheist, but he still has enough faith to believe abject nonsense. And how glibly the fantasies of faith sweep aside the terrible realities of suffering and pain. Never mind. All will be well when Christ returns.

I'm not sure what the same Christians who subscribe to such a bizarre view of the world or salvation, think when they watch David Attenborough BBC TV specials on the natural world and life on earth, or Brian Cox documentaries on *The Wonders of the Universe* or *Human Universe*. Do they dismiss these popular television documentaries and associated books as the work of wrong-headed atheists undermining their Christian worldview? And if they are more liberal-minded Christians, do they not sometimes feel challenged to revise their faith-constructs in the light of such shows? I always recommend Neil deGrasse Tyson's television series, *Cosmos: A Spacetime Odyssey* (2013), a worthy successor to Carl Sagan's original TV series, *Cosmos*, but I understand that particular series raised not a few evangelical hackles in the United States when it was released. Personally I find *Cosmos* far more inspiring than any book of Genesis and people like Cox far better informed than Moses or Saint Paul when it comes to telling the story of creation and life on earth.

All of this again to say, that Bible texts like 1 Corinthians 15:21-22 about Adam bringing death and Christ bringing life, may be interesting examples of ancient religious culture and belief, but tell us nothing about the truth of who we are, where we come from, why we suffer or what we can expect from life. I am an atheist today, not because I didn't try hard enough to believe in and serve God, but because I came to realise, as so many others have in so many different situations, the futility of recurring attempts to reconstruct a broken egg. Christianity is a broken egg.

Now I can almost hear some whit saying that broken eggs can be mended. Granted, such delicate things in the right hands can be repaired, restored, have all the pieces placed carefully back in position, but they can never be as strong again, and breaks and cracks can always be detected—ask any antique dealer. Christianity is constantly repairing itself in order to appear intact as the ground of reality shifts beneath its feet. But look closely and you'll see the cracks, and don't press it too hard, or else it will shatter. Millions of adults and young people are leaving the Church every year and they'll tell you that they don't have to be experts to see the cracks in the edifice they once thought divine.

Roman Catholic theologian Hans Kung has concluded what too many of his fellow Christians have stubbornly refused to conclude, as they rationalise that there can still be some convincing correlation between the Bible's story of human origins and sin and the story told by science. The implication of such a conclusion must always be that the traditional view of the cross of Christ and his atoning sacrifice can no longer be maintained and appears to be 'nonsense.'

> The idea of an 'original sin' handed down by sexual procreation—which does not appear either in the Hebrew Bible or in the New Testament, but was propagated by the church father Augustine (and because of which the newborn had to be baptized!)—can no longer be maintained, because there never was this human couple who sinned for all humankind. The theologian and Teilhard specialist Karl Schmitz-Moorman is right in saying: 'The classical theory of redemption is imprisoned in a static view of the world in which to begin with everything was good, and in which evil first came into the world through human beings. The notion of this traditional view of redemption as reconciliation and ransom from the consequences of Adam's fall is nonsense for anyone who knows about the evolutionary background to human existence in the modern world.'[10]

We began this book with that quintessential New Testament text, John 3:16-18: 'For God so loved the world that he gave his only Son, so that everyone who believes in him may not perish but may have eternal life. ... Those who believe in him are not condemned; but those who do not believe are condemned already.' We've dealt with the dilemma part that the verse suggests. Humans are lost, destined to perish, but God loves us so he has sent his son. Through him we can have eternal life. Let's look now more closely at the phrase, 'those who believe in him are not condemned.'

My contention is that humans are not lost, they're just human and being imperfect and 'sinful' is an inevitable part of the human condition. We are conditioned by millions of years of evolution. Humans are also capable of much goodness, even nobility and that applies to those who are non-religious just as much as it does to those who are religious—perhaps even more so. There is no God who forgives human frailty and 'sin'. We have to deal with those things ourselves. But my argument in part is that even if there were a god, why must it be Paul's God or the God of New Testament Christianity?

Whatever the consequences of his death on the cross, that death has changed nothing. It has not brought a better world. It has not abolished sin or evil, or even alleviated it. It has not ushered in a new age of peace—as the Messiah is predicted to do—and a new world or creation is still awaited. Christianity deals with this anomaly by insisting that all these things God's Messiah is meant to accomplish will be accomplished at the *second* coming of Christ. Meanwhile we have to take their word for it, that our sins are forgiven because Christ died on the cross. How do we know that is true? Because of the resurrection three days after the crucifixion. Such a 'glorious' event, celebrated every Easter is an expression of faith and hope, but after two thousand years, that hope that he is alive and coming back 'soon', as the New Testament says (Revelation 22;20)—is wearing thin. Jesus was not, as Judaism consistently recognizes, the expected Messiah or deliverer.

The religion established in his name is not the religion Jesus himself lived by and died in. Christianity was not a 'fulfilment' of biblical religion, but rather the creation of a new religious system. It would probably be news to Jesus that the religion he sought to revitalise in the spirit of the prophets and his announcement of the coming of the 'kingdom' or new age predicted by the prophets which he fervently believed in, eventually gave way to a new religion which he would not recognize. Certainly his own insistence that he had *not* come to 'abolish the Law' (Matthew 5:17-20), Judaism's law of Moses, runs counter to any idea that Judaism could be renewed by abandoning it altogether.

The colossal fiction that the human race is 'lost' and can only be restored through the sacrifice of God's Son, has been, for two thousand years, the persistent message of the Christian religion. By creating an extreme dilemma—universal estrangement from God through 'original sin'—Christianity proposes an extreme solution or cure, the sacrificial death of a first-century Jew. It is an extreme solution, for by its nature it disposes of a solution open to all—repentance as sufficient in itself, and makes Christianity the sole, exclusive avenue of salvation, the only religion with a saviour.

A great and compelling voice of reason was heard in Nineteenth century America. Heralded as perhaps the greatest orator of his age, Robert G. Ingersoll (1833-1899), the 'Great Agnostic', publicly declared that:

> If we wish to reform the world we must rely on truth, on fact, on reason. We must teach men that they are good or bad for themselves, that others cannot be good or bad for them, that they cannot be charged with the crimes, or credited with the virtues of others. We must discard the doctrine of the atonement, because it is absurd and immoral. We are not accountable for the sins of 'Adam' and the virtues of Christ cannot be transferred to us. There can be no vicarious virtue, no vicarious vice. Why should the sufferings of the innocent atone for the crimes of the guilty... We do not need the forgiveness of gods, but of ourselves and the ones we injure. Restitution without repentance is far better than repentance without restitution.'[11]

We need evangelists of reason to conduct such crusades today as Ingersoll did in America more than a century and a half ago.

Down the Rabbit Hole– Part 1

Explaining Salvation:
'down the rabbit hole', a metaphor for an entry into the unknown, the disorientating or the mentally deranging, from its use in 'Alice's Adventures in Wonderland'

In this chapter I want to examine the different ways in which some Christian theologians—Robert Brinsmead, John Stott, Jean Calvin and I. Howard Marshall—have tried to explain and defend the doctrine of the Atonement or Christian salvation. It ought to become increasingly evident that the more Christian theologians explain their view of salvation, the deeper the hole of incomprehensibility they dig. We are then left wondering how such perverse fantasy ever become a major world religion?

Robert D. Brinsmead (1933 –) became a controversial figure within the Seventh-day Adventist Church in the 1960s and 1970s. He eventually broke with Adventism and became a strong advocate of the more mainstream Protestant principle of 'justification by faith alone,' drawing on the writings of Martin Luther and other Protestant reformers. He founded the magazine *Present Truth,* whose name was later changed to *Verdict*. In the days when

I was a young minister, fervently devoted to the Protestant Reformed (Calvinistic) faith, I devoured issues of this magazine and applauded the contribution they were making to expounding the 'true' faith. Brinsmead was on a spiritual journey which continued beyond Verdict and his theology became more radical, far less conservative. Eventually he appeared to reject many orthodox Christian teachings, seeing God's dealings with humankind as being much broader than the narrative contained in the Bible. In the 1990s he seemed to drop out of the church scene altogether and became involved in politics and his tropical fruit theme park in northern coastal New South Wales. Currently Brinsmead though still a theist, is more humanist in his writings.

In one of the further ironies of my own spiritual journey, I came across the website of Robert D. Brinsmead at the end of 2012. I had been 'googling' through articles on the Atonement and purely by chance, came across an article by Brinsmead. I read a number of his online essays and was so intrigued by his journey away from orthodoxy that I wrote to him and we exchanged several emails. One of the things I said in my first email was: 'For me, and obviously you have noted it too, blood-atonement is crucial to Christianity and once the whole concept of a substitutionary death is abandoned, the need for a 'Savior' must also be re-assessed. I could no longer believe that Christianity was an improvement on Judaism, when the 'Old' Testament clearly taught that God forgives sin on the basis of sincere repentance. ... Judaism is not exclusive but believes that the righteous of every faith will have a place in heaven. You know how exclusivist Christianity is by contrast.' (my email dated 6 December, 2012). At the time I wrote that to Brinsmead, I still had one whole year to go as minister of my last church.

I mention Brinsmead because he is a fine example of an articulate, Christian scholar and lay-theologian in Australia who passionately promoted the orthodox faith, but eventually found it unsustainable. His Verdict magazine was distributed worldwide by Brinsmead and his associates for almost twenty-five years. Its central theme was 'The Gospel plus nothing and nothing but the Gospel'. Those who followed his arguments then, could profit from reading his essays since. One such essay, dealing with the topics of the Fall, Hell and Atonement by blood sacrifice is called, Excursus on the Chamber of Horrors. In it he states that, 'The Fall is the beginning of the story. The story has a Hell of an end. In the middle is Atonement by means of a blood sacrifice. From beginning to end it is a Chamber of Horrors. It is totally incompatible with the life and teaching of Joshua ben Adam.' (his re-naming of Jesus Christ). Brinsmead regards the Christian story of the cross of Christ as a 're-cycled pagan myth.' I recommend the essay. He who so passionately defended the Christian theory of atonement before, has come to see its absurdity and even its horror.

> We also need to confront the serious fallacies conveyed in this very foundational story. In the first place, it is completely erroneous to suggest that any human sin (least of all one misdemeanor) brought all the disruption and death into this world. Millions of years before any man walked this earth there was upheavals, wholesale destruction of species, and enough death going on in the world to make rivers of fossil fuel.
> Secondly, if God is the author of life he is also the author of death. There could have been no development and improvement of any species without death. To put on mankind the responsibility for causing death is not only an appalling burden, but it is both harmful and false.
> The worst aspect of the story, however, is that it conveys a concept of retributive (pay-back) justice so horrific that it defies even the rudiments of good sense. For one misdemeanor a man and women lost paradise for themselves and the entire human race. The punishment was suffering and death not just for themselves but for billions of other people for millennium after millennium.[1]

He is particularly disturbed by the Christian doctrine of Hell and eternal punishment, a doctrine which many Christians—usually of a liberal persuasion—have also rejected. 'With Hell, God's pay-back justice takes on infinite proportions. Sin is said to be an offence against an infinite majesty meriting infinite punishment. So God spends eternity getting even, paying people back for offending him.' With the same clarity he used to describe the orthodox doctrine of the atonement, Brinsmead now reminds us of the obvious flaws in the doctrine.

> The transaction is said to be *substitutionary*. Christ, the innocent one, was treated as we deserved that we, the guilty ones, might be treated as he deserves. God rolled on him the sins of the world and punished him as if he were every sinner. (It is said that Christ's human nature was sustained by his divine nature to endure an infinite punishment making a sufficient atonement for the sins of the world).
>
> If it be asked, 'Why was this atonement necessary?' the answer is that God could not forgive sin unless he satisfied his law or his principle of retributive justice. Anselm said that reparations or an adequate compensation had to be made to God's outraged honor due to man's sin.
>
> The real reason God offers the bloody sacrifice of his son and Christ offers himself as the victim, therefore, is not to save people but it is to justify the divine administration, to satisfy God's justice, to honor and glorify God, etc. ... Christ died primarily for the principle of law and pay-back justice. If God cannot forgive us unless Christ pays our debt, then he does not really forgive at all. If a debt has been paid, then there is nothing to forgive. Atonement and forgiveness, therefore, are mutually exclusive.[2]

Brinsmead's final point is insightful and, I believe, unanswerable. Judaism understands what he is saying. Christianity does not, or will not. The concept that forgiveness without first having to punish is not really forgiveness, is what again, constitutes Christianity's Achilles Heel. Saint Anselm of Canterbury (c. 1033 – 21 April 1109), a Benedictine monk, philosopher, and prelate of the Church, who held the office of Archbishop of Canterbury from 1093 to 1109, was the founder of Christian 'scholasticism'. He has been a major influence in Western theology and is famous as the originator of the *ontological* argument for the existence of God and the *satisfaction theory of atonement*.

The reader needs to remember that there have been a number of theories of the atonement, not one of which has won the universal assent of the whole Christian world. In other words, no one can entirely make sense of it. Nevertheless, Anselm's theory demonstrates a plausible interpretation of the theology of Saint Paul, but also demonstrates how much theology has had to depend on creative imagination in order to defend such indefensible concepts as the atonement.

According to St. Anselm God's forgiveness is not possible through sheer mercy but only by rendering the appropriate *satisfaction* to God's wounded honour and holiness. Anselm considered man's offence against God to be of an 'infinite' nature—a rather harsh assessment—and therefore one which required an 'infinite' satisfaction. What human being or group of humans could possibly offer God an infinite satisfaction? None of course. Brinsmead again reminds us that we really need to think about what we believe forgiveness is.

> Does the God who insists that the debt be paid in full before he extends his forgiveness really forgive at all? One can demand that a debt be paid or one can forgive the debt, but doing both is mutually exclusive. Yet according to Christian teaching, Christ died 'making it possible for God to offer pardon to sinners.'[3]

Hans Kung, the renowned and often controversial German Catholic theologian, has observed that, 'What is dominant in this theory is not New Testament grace, mercy and love, but, as in Roman Law, justice understood in a very human way. For the sake of logic, Jesus' death on the cross is isolated from his message and life and at the same time also from his resurrection: essentially Jesus came simply to die. It is a deadly illusory performance between father and Son or indeed between the divine and human nature in the Son, based on legal niceties.'[4] Kung represents a kinder, more liberal Christian theology of the Cross, though it is difficult to see how even a liberal view fully makes sense of Christ's death, or how we are to understand 'New Testament grace, mercy and love' as we contemplate the Cross.

Is Christ simply a martyr after all, willing to suffer the ultimate penalty for speaking the 'truth' and seeking to help his fellow human beings? In moments of great doubt about my Christian faith, I often found Kung helpful and re-assuring. The liberal view of Christianity is certainly more palatable and easier to live with. But as I have said before, the basic texts of the Christian religion do not really give us permission to stray very far from its harsh realities. I think this is evident in Kung's analysis of the doctrine of the atonement. It also hints at why successive popes have withdrawn his license to teach theology in Catholic seminaries.

> The Satisfaction Theory reflects not so much the New Testament as the Middle Ages. But what was the original message of the Cross? If an up-to-date understanding of redemption has to be freed from juridical and cultic constrains, must not the concept of sacrifice also be abandoned? Can there be any doubt that the concept of *expiatory sacrifice* in particular—in popular exposition at least—often creates really painful misunderstandings, linked as it is with pagan sacrifice? Is God so cruel, even sadistic, that his anger can be appeased only by the blood of his Son? Does an innocent person have to act as a scapegoat, whipping boy and substitute for the real sinners?
>
> It cannot be disputed that the apostolic proclamation—perhaps following Jesus' own interpretation—sees Jesus death as expiatory— as sign of reconciliation, as slaughtered Passover lamb, as Lamb of God who bears the sins of the world. But only in Hebrews, written by an unknown Hellenistic author, partly utilizing Pauline motifs, is the theme of sacrifice broadly developed in cultic terminology: as a radical criticism of the Jewish cult. … . Jesus 'sacrifice' must in fact *not* be understood in the *Old Testament and pagan sense.*[5]

Try as he might, and much as I once wanted him to be correct, it is clear from this quotation that the only way to be freed from 'the concept of expiatory sacrifice' is simply to insist that it 'must *not* be understood in the *Old Testament and pagan sense.*' My problem in my struggles with the faith was that I could not find any liberal explanation for Christ's death on the cross that ultimately made sense, or could honestly be said to be derived from Scripture. You either accepted the traditional view or, as I concluded, abandon Christianity altogether because that view remains 'unethical and unbelievable', and Judaism really hasn't been improved on. Why didn't we just stay Jewish in the first century?

Kung does suggest that in the context of an ancient, more primitive religious world, the idea of sacrifice did not seem at all odd. Today, he suggests, sacrifice is not related to any experience that we observe and has thus 'become largely misleading and unintelligible'. He even goes so far as to state his opinion that: 'the concept of the sacrifice of the Mass today is even more problematic'.[6] A towering theologian of the Roman Catholic Church is suggesting that the central, most significant sacrament of the Church needs to be thought of in terms other than that of sacrifice. But the Catholic Mass is so inextricably linked to the concept of sacrifice that it is hard to understand how else it could be presented.

For centuries Catholics have participated in what they consider to be the 'sacrifice of the Mass'. The Catechism of the Catholic Church clearly states that: 'This sacrament is called the 'Holy sacrifice', because it makes present the one sacrifice of Christ the Saviour and includes the Church's offering. . . It completes and surpasses all the sacrifices of the Old Covenant.'[7] Kung may think its terminology misleading and unintelligible, but the Church's understanding is unambiguous. 'The Eucharist is thus a sacrifice because it re-presents (makes present) the sacrifice of the cross ... The sacrifice of Christ and the sacrifice of the Eucharist are *one single sacrifice:* 'The victim is one and the same: the same now offers through the ministry of priests, who then offered himself on the cross; only the manner of offering is different.' 'And since in the divine sacrifice which is celebrated in the Mass, the same Christ who offered himself once in a bloody manner on the altar of the cross is contained and offered in an unbloody manner ... . this sacrifice is truly propitiatory*' (*intended to atone for ; appease, placate God).[8]

If Kung finds this historic, traditional concept 'misleading' and 'unintelligible' imagine how the Jews have always found it, and how non-believers today find it. Few have attempted alternative ways of understanding traditional dogma better than Kung, but like all theists he is committed to making sense of nonsense and that is not an enviable task. The death of Christ is difficult to understand, so he reminds us that it is the resurrection that vindicates Christ and makes his suffering somehow bearable and worthwhile. These are his words:

> It is now clearer than ever that the God manifested in Jesus is not a cruel, despotic, legal-minded God, but a God encountering man as redeeming love, identifying himself in Jesus with suffering man. .... He is a God who unlike the pagan gods does not take his revenge on those who sin against him ... He is a God who lavishes his grace on those who do not deserve it. It follows from all this that the cross is not to be understood as a sacrifice demanded by a cruel God. In the light of Easter it was understood as quite the reverse, as the deepest expression of his love—love, not as feeling, but as 'existing for', 'doing good to' others. A love that is, which cannot be defined abstractly but only with reference to this Jesus.[9]

But 'a God who lavishes his grace on those who do not deserve it' is precisely the God we encounter in the Old Testament, the God who forgives out of 'sheer mercy'. That, at least, was King David's experience. Jews in the first century and now would say that they need no cross to convince them of God's love. Their scriptures are filled with praise of that love. And how, in Kung's words, can the cross be 'the deepest expression of God's love' when it involves the terrible suffering of a man who, at the end, cries out 'My God! My God! Why have you forsaken me?' The crucifixion and death of Christ is not, as Christians assert, the central 'mystery' of the Christian faith. Dressing it up in mystery doesn't make it any more respectable or credible. Any theory which makes human forgiveness and salvation dependent on satisfying the wounded honour of an imaginary god must be rejected as a primitive and irrational notion.

When explaining what we suspect is unexplainable, Christian theologians, particularly of the conservative tradition, raise more questions than they answer. Two examples worth considering are explanations of the atonement by the late John Stott, and the website of Anglicans of the Sydney, Australia diocese. First to Stott, minister of All Souls Langham Place London for many years. John Stott, an Englishman, was one of the Twentieth-century's key Evangelical Protestant figures, a prominent and articulate leader in that tradition of Christianity. During my ministry I owned most of his books and was greatly influenced in my preaching by his teaching and exposition of scripture. He died in July 2011, lauded as the closest thing to an evangelical pope.

Those evangelicals who resented the growing tide of theologians and pastors questioning the traditional doctrine of substitutionary atonement, found a champion in John Stott. One of the classic expositions of the doctrine can be read in his book *The Cross of Christ*, first published in 1986. The 20th anniversary edition was published in 2006. Stott relentlessly places Jesus' self-substitution at the center of redemption. While engaged in a deeper study of the atonement during my period of increasing disaffection with the faith, I wrote some responsive notes on the content of this book. I include here a selection of his statements in italics, followed by my responses.

1. Instead of inflicting upon us the judgment we deserved, God in Christ endured it in our place. Hell is the only alternative. This is the 'scandal', the stumbling block of the cross. For our proud hearts rebel against it. We cannot bear to acknowledge either the seriousness of our sin and guilt or our utter indebtedness to the cross.[10]

Response: We all, without exception, apparently deserve death. Since Christ took our place on the cross, dying a particularly gruesome death, then that is obviously what God thinks we all deserve. Not only physical death in the form of a punishment, but then eternal separation and pain hereafter. Though God seems so convinced that we deserve death, he also loves us, and so in order to save us from that death and endless separation, he bears that punishment himself! Of course we have already been condemned to die, not just because that it an inevitable part of the natural order of the world, but because we are descended from the 'first' two humans, Adam and Eve, whose sin has been transmitted to us all. Everyone deserves this punishment that Christ suffered on our behalf, even little children, wise Greek philosophers, ordinary, decent-living citizens of the Roman Empire at the time this was written, not to mention Gandhi and the Buddha—everyone.

Everyone has offended God just be having the sinful nature they have, and that offence can only be forgiven through a blood sacrifice entailing a gruesome, drawn-out death on a cross. Stott at least is correct in saying that 'we cannot bear to acknowledge the seriousness of our sin and guilt.' He says our 'pride' prevents us, but perhaps it is more likely our common-sense, our sense of proportion, justice and understanding of human nature that shrinks from the idea that we are all so sinful and guilty that we deserve death!

2. We insist on paying for what we have done. We cannot stand the humiliation of acknowledging our bankruptcy and allowing somebody else to pay for us. The notion that this somebody else should be God himself is just too much to take. We would rather perish than repent, rather lose ourselves than humble ourselves. [11]

Response: It would never naturally occur to anyone that God himself should pay for the things *we* do wrong. Only we can do that. And the only way we can avoid paying for our sins is to repent of them, as Judaism so ably shows us; as the Bible shows us. The only reason such a preposterous idea ever entered the religious world, was because the early Christians had to make sense of Christ's unexpected death. They did that—at least St. Paul did—by saying that Jesus had died for our sins and since Jesus was God incarnate, then God himself died for our sins.

Christian theologians have always struggled with that one. Jesus is God they affirm, but God the Father didn't die on the cross, only God the Son. (It is actually a heresy from the earliest Christian centuries called *patripassionism* to think that God the Father died on the cross). Yes, there is only *one* God, but there are distinctions or 'persons' within the Godhead. The Son dies for us, not the Father. Jews and most people with a normal brain struggle to understand how you can believe in one God, but insist that there are three, co-equal, eternally existing 'persons' who make up that one God. This is the 'Trinity' of course, but Christianity has never been able to explain that doctrine to anyone's satisfaction either. So while God remained in heaven or wherever he is supposed to be, an extension of God which had become a human being, hung and died on the cross. That extension, the 'Son', cried out 'My God, my God, why have you forsaken me!?' It is not pride that makes this hard for us to understand. It is simply unbelievable.

And as for Stott saying that 'we would rather perish than repent', that is simply not true. There are numerous texts in the Old Testament indicating that God positively encouraged people to repent—and they did. See: Psalm 34:18, Jonah 3:7-10, Proverbs 16:6, 21:13, 28:13, Micah 6:6-8 and 2 Chronicles 7:14. The Chronicles text in particular is one which Christians are very fond of quoting and applying to themselves and their 'Christian' nations, despite the fact that it is addressed specifically to Israel. In this text, God reassures his people that if they 'humble themselves, pray, seek my face, and turn from their wicked ways (*teshuvah* or repentance), then I will hear from heaven, and will *forgive their sin* and heal their land.' And he forgave them. They didn't perish. Another, if not the most profound and moving example of God's response to repentance is King David's repentance in Psalm 51.

3. Galatians 3:10-14, 'Christ became a curse for us'. The language here is startling, almost shocking. We should not have dared to use it ... Nevertheless the apostle Paul did use this language ... We need to feel the logic of Paul's teaching. First, all who rely on the law are under a curse. At the beginning of verse 10 Paul again uses the expression 'all who rely on observing the law.' The reason Paul can declare such to be 'under a curse' is that Scripture says they are: 'Cursed is everyone who does not continue to do everything written in the Book of the Law' (Deuteronomy 27:26). No human being has ever continued to do 'everything' the law requires. Such a continuous and comprehensive obedience has been given by no one except Jesus. [12]

Response: Stott's reasoning here is common in Christian thinking but it betrays a persisting Christian misunderstanding about the Jewish 'Law' or Torah. Jews believed in Jesus' day, as they do today, that they receive God's favour or 'grace' immediately from God, without a mediator. They believe that *God* is the Saviour of Israel, that they are saved by his grace and mercy. They obey the Law, love the law, extol the Law, because it is a 'tree of life' according to Scripture, not because it saves them, but because they are already 'saved.'. The Law or Torah tells them *how* to live and it is do-able. The apostle Paul always argued that only Christ can save, not the law. But Judaism never said that the law saved them. People can't fully keep the law, so they are condemned, Paul says, but the God of the Old Testament understands human nature and is wise enough not to expect perfection of his creatures. He condemns no one for being imperfect. Paul wants to replace Judaism with his new version of salvation through Christ, so he twists the Old Testament concept of the Law into something it never claimed to be.

Example: the Old Testament book of Deuteronomy 30: 1-16, has God exhorting the children of Israel to keep the Law, keep the commandments. He clearly indicates that such obedience is well within their reach and ability.

Surely, this commandment that I am commanding you today *is not too hard for you* (which it would be if they had to keep it perfectly). It is not up in heaven that you should say, 'Who will go up to heaven for us, and get is for us that we may hear it and observe it?' Neither is it beyond the sea that you should say, 'Who will cross to the other side of the sea for us and get it for us so that we may hear it and observe it?' No, the word is very near to you; it is in your mouth and in your heart for you to observe. ... choose life so that you and your descendants may live.'

When Paul in the New Testament presents an argument for his own peculiar version of salvation, he refers to this same text but gives it a completely different spin. He says that Moses was talking about 'the righteousness that comes from the law' and he contrasts that with the 'righteousness that comes from faith'—faith in Christ. The 'word' that is near them he says, the word that is 'on your lips and in your heart' is no longer the Torah or commandments of God that Deuteronomy spoke of, it is 'the word of faith ... because if you confess with your lips that Jesus is Lord and believe in your heart that God raised him from the dead, you will be saved' (Romans 10:5-9). He first creates a straw man of salvation—the Jewish Law—and then demolishes it, replacing it with the person and saving work of Christ. The 'all' who are under the law are obviously the Jews and they are under a 'curse'. This is a very negative, but very Christian view of the Jewish Law.

Paul is suggesting that the law only shows people that they are incapable of keeping it. They are condemned for that inability. According to him, these laws were apparently given by God to teach the Jews that they were incapable of keeping the law or commandments, and that because they could not keep the law, they were cursed by it. Paul tells them that they would eventually need the saving death of Jesus on the cross to give them true forgiveness of sins. This really is a bizarre way of thinking. Why would God give his people laws he knew they could not keep? Does the passage in Deuteronomy suggest he thought they couldn't keep them? No. And then why would he curse or condemn them for not being able to fully keep the laws he gave them?

Judaism cannot conceive of a God who would be so unreasonable, cruel and lacking in compassion. Paul obviously could. Besides, if you look at Deuteronomy 27:6 where it refers to the 'curse', it is not saying that anyone who does not keep *all* the commandments of the Law of Moses will be cursed, but that 'Cursed be anyone who does not uphold the words of *this* law by observing them.' What is *this* law? Well it is a specific list of laws outlined in the second half of the chapter, laws that concern idolatry, dishonouring of parents, cheating neighbours, misleading blind people, depriving the alien, the orphan and the widow of justice, committing incest, taking bribes etc., Christianity has made an art form of saying what the Jewish scriptures do *not* say.

Stott rightly senses that we are offended by Paul's language. The idea that Christ became a 'curse' for us or that God 'made him to be sin who knew no sin, so that in him we might become the righteousness of God' (Second Corinthians 5:21), is clearly 'startling', 'shocking' indeed. Jesus is being made like us, identifying with us in our sinful condition, suffering the just punishment of a sinner on the cross. When we remember that this Christ is also supposed to be God himself incarnate, it is all too difficult to understand—and cannot be understood in any rational way. This is a wild, imaginative construct of the mind of Paul. It made no sense to Judaism.

Stott's final sentence that 'such a continuous and comprehensive obedience has been given by no one except Jesus' re-iterates the Christian idea that God expects perfection of us and that all are condemned *because they are imperfect*. It doesn't really help to say, well, Christ was perfect, so if you believe in him and accept that he died in your place, then God will overlook your imperfection and grant you salvation. We ought not to be interested in such a solution when it is clear that the problem has been grossly misrepresented in the first place. As Max Brod once wrote: 'In order to point out the need for Christ's atoning death, man's fall, which preceded it—the original sin—is painted in the most horrifying colours.'[13]

4. 'How then could God express simultaneously his holiness in judgment and his love in pardon? Only by providing a divine substitute for the sinner, so that the substitute would receive the judgment and the sinner the pardon.'[14]

Response: Or he could just forgive? This is a New Testament concept imposed on the Old (Jewish) Testament. The Jewish Scriptures say that God does actually express both holiness and judgment and love in pardon. Time after time he simply forgives the repentant without any mention of having to punish a substitute. How is it forgiveness, if it still exacts a price, if holy judgment must be satisfied by some offering?

5. 'The deserved penalty of alienation from God has been borne by another in our place.' [Stott here quotes E.B. Cranfield as having given the best explanation of Romans 3:25: 'God, because in his mercy he willed to forgive sinful men, and being truly merciful, willed to forgive them righteously, that is, without in any way condoning their sin', (so far so good, but then Cranfield adds ...) purposed to direct against his very own self in the person of his Son the full weight of that righteous wrath which they deserved'. ... 'It is impossible for the blood of bulls and goats to take away sin' (New Testament book of Hebrews 9:22). Animal sacrifice could not atone for human beings ... only the precious blood of Christ was valuable enough.[15]

Response: In the Old Testament God repeatedly does what Cranfield states in the first part of his explanation, but never suggests the second part. If he had, the Jews and the rest of the world would have been better prepared for the Christian religion which came afterwards. It is absurd that God would do such a thing, would need to do such a thing—to himself!—when he can simply forgive. The Christian text to which Stott refers attempts to point out the ineffectiveness of (Jewish) animal sacrifice by suggesting that it only made sense as a preparation or prefigurement of the human sacrifice of Christ to come, a sacrifice that would be effective in achieving forgiveness. This implies that *human* sacrifice is necessary for atonement, something God explicitly forbids in the Old Testament (despite the story of Abraham and Isaac). The non-believer would hear something like this and conclude that neither animal nor human sacrifice achieves anything. In fact the whole notion of sacrifice is primitive and wrong.

I have always found it intriguing that the one founder of a major world religion who *didn't* believe in God or revelation—Buddha, also didn't believe in sacrifices. In his time and culture the Hindu deities of India were offered animal sacrifices just as the Hebrew God was. It's a fairly common practice in most religions. Yet the Buddha who achieved 'enlightenment' and never claimed to have received his wisdom or insights from any divine source, considered sacrifices to be vulgar, cruel and useless. 'All these rites are not worth a sixteenth part of having a heart filled with love, any more than the radiance of the moon outshines the stars'.[16]

How is it that Buddha, for all intents and purposes, a practicing atheist, thought of sacrifices as vulgar, cruel and useless, yet the God of the Jews did not? It is true in the time of the prophets, that the emphasis changed, so that their sentiments approximated those of the Buddha, but one of the obvious arguments against the existence of God—at least the one in the Bible—is that he instituted such vulgarity, cruelty and uselessness as part of the Law he 'revealed' to Moses.

Judaism, as I have tried to demonstrate, is a very effective foil to Christianity, but it certainly has its own problems when it comes to things like sacrifice. I was drawn to it initially because it made more sense than Christianity, but it remains a religion which still gives evidence of being a human invention, a creation of our evolving religious imagination. Though most Jews today regard the ancient site of the Temple in Jerusalem as a 'sacred' place, they are glad they are not part of that form of Judaism that centred on the glorified, religious abattoir that was still the Temple in Jesus' time.

What concerns me about the more orthodox elements in Judaism today is that they still subscribe to the mentality of animal sacrifices. Even Rabbi Shmuley Boteach, a man who has debated and discussed Jesus and Christianity with leading Christian scholars for more than twenty years, and is regarded by some as 'the most famous rabbi in America', looks forward to a time when the Temple will be restored! 'The prophet Ezekiel makes it clear sacrifices will resume with the rebuilding of the Third Temple (yet future). He describes tables on which the burnt offerings, sin offerings and guilt offerings were slaughtered ... Clearly, once the Third Temple comes to be, sacrificial practice will return to the ways of the First Temple. Thus, even if we were to accept Christian theologian's' claim that Jesus' martyrdom replaced sacrifices in the absence of the Second Temple (Herod's), this sacrifice would be eclipsed by the Third Temple—in a stroke, *instantly making Christianity obsolete.*' (emphasis mine).[17]

Boteach's expectation is further strengthened by the existence of the 'Temple Institute' in Jerusalem today, where *cohanin* or priests are being trained to perform the sacrifices and the very instruments of Temple worship and sacrifice are being reproduced. (Google it if you don't believe me). Bizarrely, as I mentioned before, a lot of American Evangelical Christians support such a project and would like to donate towards its costs (not permissible under Jewish law) because they believe that the rebuilding of the Temple in Jerusalem is another preparatory sign heralding the second coming of Christ. In their enthusiasm for the fulfillment of 'prophecy' they do not seem to grasp that such a project, if brought to fruition, would, in Boteach's words result in 'instantly making Christianity obsolete.' That surely would be the final irony in this long difficult relationship between Judaism and Christianity.

6. 'It is one and the same God who through Christ saves us from himself' (166). Stott describes how the divine judge assumes the role of the innocent victim. *'There is only (here) unfathomable mystery'.*[18]

Response: Indeed, but a mystery of man's making. Is this really comprehensible or is it absurdity? Penal or substitutionary atonement means *poenia* (Greek)—a penalty or punishment. God saves us from himself by punishing himself. We are supposed to believe in a God who loves us and yet the only way that loving God can prevent his wrath over our sin from destroying us is to punish himself! Though not exactly 'himself' because it his 'son' Jesus who dies in agony on the cross. But Jesus *is* God, though not God the Father. But we are not allowed to conclude that there are two gods, only one.

Jurgen Moltmann in his book with the rather confusing title, *The Crucified God,* writes that 'we cannot say that the father also suffered and died. The suffering and dying of the Son, forsaken by the father, is a different kind of suffering from the suffering of the father in the death of the Son. Nor can the death of Jesus be understood in theopaschite terms as the 'death of God".[19] Most Christian congregations are not filled with theologians, so you can imagine how difficult it is for ministers preparing their Good Friday sermons to make all of this seem believable to their people.

Surprisingly most congregations just accept the narrative, sing the Easter hymns that give them emotional reinforcement and try not to think too deeply about it all. Jesus died for their sins and that is all that matters. Who could not be moved and appreciative of that? Occasionally someone might ask a question about how it works really and you just had to reassure them that God's word assures us that it does, even if we don't understand how. Previously we analyzed the classic Christian text John 3:16. It began with the phrase, 'For God so love the world that *he gave his only Son ...*' . Christians must have recited or read those words thousands of times but never really stopped to reflect on how absurd it is to believe that there is only one God, *and* that that one God gave his only Son who is supposed to be God, to die for us. No wonder groups like the Mormons, claiming to be Christian, reject the doctrine of the Trinity altogether and accept the plain, common-sense teaching of the New Testament that God the Father and Jesus Christ are two separate and individual beings. It is a concept with far more New Testament verses to back it up than any concept of a Trinity.

In writing his epistles, the apostle Paul often begins by greeting the churches with the blessing, 'Grace to you and peace from God our Father *and* the Lord Jesus Christ' (1 Corinthians 1:3). Still, Christians cannot accept this easy way out of their theological dilemmas for that would mean abandoning the link with Judaism and its belief in *one* God. Having made that decision, they must continue to attempt explanations for their inconsistent and contradictory beliefs. Consider Jurgen Moltmann's attempt at explaining what was happening on the cross when Jesus, feeling abandoned by God, cried out in despair.

> What happened on the cross was an event between God and God. It was a deep division in God himself, in so far as God abandoned God and contradicted himself, and at the same time a unity in God, in so far as God was at one with God and corresponded to himself. One would have to put the formula in a paradoxical way: God died the death of the godless (humans) on the cross and yet did not die. God is dead and yet is not dead.[20]

What can any reasonable person say in response to a statement like that? This text of Moltmann's was one of our standard texts in Theology at theological college studying for the ministry. No wonder Christians scratch their heads about stuff like this. I have discovered that some of the most effective arguments against the existence of a god or gods come from Buddhist writers, inspired by the teachings of the Buddha himself. Gunapala Dharmasiri wrote *A Buddhist Critique of the Christian Concept of God* in 1974. He talks about the talk of the Hindu Brahmins versed in the Vedas turning out to be 'ridiculous, mere words, a vain and empty thing!' and then goes on to apply that assessment to Christianity.

> When the concept of God is not meaningfully established, the Buddha said, it becomes pointless to build a religion or a religious language based on the concept of God. If the central concept is meaningless then the whole edifice of religion and the path of salvation are equally meaningless.
>
> The Buddha maintained that the clear meaningfulness of terms and concepts was an indispensable factor for clear thinking and understanding of things. Without clear terms and concepts one could not think in any intelligible way. 'God' is the most central concept on which rests the whole philosophy and religion of Christianity. If that concept is surrounded by a mass of philosophical and religious problems which render it practically meaningless, it points to the fragility of the foundations of Christianity as a religion. ... It is not surprising that the theological reflections of Christianity are essentially unclear and obscure.[21]

This is a profoundly different approach to the question of truth than the Christian approach which insists on propagating mysteries beyond our comprehension. John 3:16 spoke of God so loving the world, yet we have seen that a forgiveness that cannot be offered until some satisfaction or punishment is levied, is a strange expression of love. This is why Dharmasiri spoke of the god-concept 'dying the death of a thousand qualifications.'

> Thus ultimately 'love' loses its meaning and so the idea of 'God who loves' becomes meaningless. This way of making frustrating qualifications is the theologian's method of avoiding the contradictions inherent in the doctrine of God ... That is why most of Christian theological thinking is very inconsistent. The theologians, when challenged, immediately start qualifying.[22]

It is this realization that leads some Christians to reject their faith. They grow tired of the meaningless chatter and the endless qualifications and contradictions.

7. He (Jesus) would be pierced for our transgressions, the Lord would lay on him the iniquity of us all, that he would thus be numbered with the transgressors, and that he would himself bear their iniquities ... J.S. Whale wrote 'that the servant suffers the penalty of other men's sins: not only vicarious suffering but penal substitution is the plain meaning of the verses. [23]

Response: All human sin, lust, hate, envy, greed, selfishness, etc., would be laid on God!? Again, this is incomprehensible and to Jews and Muslims it must sound blasphemous. Why must God himself endure all of this misery, horror and degradation in order to forgive us? Where is the power he previously had in the Old Testament to forgive without punishing, a forgiveness that was the expression of his mercy and compassion rather than some absolute compulsion to satisfy his justice? Stott writes: 'It is God who must satisfy himself as holy love. He was unwilling to act in love at the expense of his holiness or in holiness at the expense of his love.'[24] Yet that is precisely what God *did* do in the Jewish Scriptures. This dilemma that Stott is trying to explain is a purely Christian quandary that has no precedent or roots in the Old Testament.

Stott quotes P.T. Forsyth saying that 'the one thing God could not do in the face of human rebellion was nothing.' He must either inflict punishment or assume it, and he chose the latter course as honouring the law by saving the guilty. He took his own judgment (upon himself).[25] Where in all of the Old Testament scriptures does it even begin to suggest that God faces such a choice? What of the many examples in those same scriptures where God witholds punishment, does not inflict it or 'assume' it—but rather *forgives* it! Is it possible that Christians really do not fully grasp the simplicity, the power, the pure grace of 'mere forgiveness' expressed by the religion of the Jews? Who is this harsh, demanding, condemning God that Paul and the New Testament have made of the God of Abraham, Isaac and Jacob? Stott and other Christian apologists know that if the Jewish view of repentance and forgiveness is correct, then the whole theology built around the cross of Jesus collapses. Explaining Salvation:

Down the Rabbit Hole– Part 2

'This God, waiting around Eden—knowing all the while
what would happen—having made them on purpose
so that it would happen, then does what?
Holds all of us responsible, and we were not there.'

– Robert G. Ingersoll

The final example in this section of how Christian theologians and organizations explain their Faith, are these excerpts from the website of the Archdiocese of Sydney Anglicans. People submit questions and staff at the Anglican Media Centre answer them. I have selected a few which are concerned with the issue of salvation.

Question: What does it mean to have your name written in the 'Book of Life'? Romans 17:8 talks about those whose names were not written in the book of life before the foundation of the world. We know that the elect's names have been written in the book of life before the foundation of the world. We also know that names can be blotted out of the book of life—Revelation 3—and there is a reference in the Psalms. My question is, are some created for hell? It appears some are elected for salvation. Of those some can choose sin and trade in the truth of God for a lie. And it seems there's another group not written in the book of life before the foundation of the world in which God is displaying his justice, while in the life of the elect he is displaying his mercy—Romans 9. Is this a sound evaluation of the holy scriptures?— Anthony.

Answer: Dear Anthony, you are certainly right to say that some are elected for salvation. Everyone destined for salvation was chosen before the foundation of the world (Ephesians 1:4), which is why Revelation 17:8 teaches that the Book of Life was written *before* the foundation of the world. Revelation 3:5 does not imply that a name can be blotted out of the book; God denies that he will blot out their names. In the Old Testament the 'book' is a little bit different. Exod. 32:33 and Psalm 69:28 do speak about the names of sinners being blotted out of the book, but there is no suggestion that this is the book of the elect; it is just the book of the living. So these Old Testament texts do not indicate that an elect person can be blotted out. No elect person can ever be blotted out of the book. And in fact, Moses asked God to blot him out for the sake of the Israelites who had sinned, and God said no; he would not blot Moses out (Exod. 32:32-33).

It is also clear that not everyone is elect. Those not written in the Book of Life will be thrown into the lake of fire (Rev. 19:15). It is going too far to say that they are created for hell. But it is true that God uses them to display his wrath (Rom. 9:22), so that we truly know that he is a consuming fire. It is so that those who are elect will stand in awe, and praise God for his amazing mercy in Christ, because we know that all people deserve to face God's wrath. The bottom line is that God predestines the elect in love, and with the purpose that they praise his glorious grace (Eph. 1:4-6). I have prayed for you, and I hope this answers helps you. Andrew.[1]

This is the official teaching of the Anglican Church of Australia, an Anglican Media Sydney production, 2014. The theology of this particular diocese, the largest and richest in the nation, is of a markedly conservative and Reformed character. They are, for example, adamantly opposed to the ordination of women to the priesthood. I cite this example, because it illustrates how one level of absurdity inevitably gives rise to a further level of absurdity.

This conservative brand of Christianity had its roots in the Sixteenth century Protestant Reformation. Martin Luther was 'Reformed' in his theology, but it was John Calvin (1509-1564) who was the formative theologian for this school of theology. Calvin was an influential French theologian and pastor during the Protestant Reformation, with his ministry centred largely in Geneva Switzerland. Calvinism is a theological orientation rather than a denomination. The Puritans were Calvinists.

Calvin was the principal architect of the system of Christian theology later called Calvinism. Reformed theology and Calvinism have become synonymous. Calvinism includes the doctrine of predestination and the absolute sovereignty of God in the salvation of human beings. Calvin's theological roots lie in the more ancient Catholic Augustinian tradition (after St. Augustine: 354—430 A.D.), and Augustine himself found his inspiration in the epistles of the apostle Paul. The Reformed and Presbyterian churches, which look to Calvin as the chief expositor of their beliefs, have, for centuries been part of mainstream Christianity and their theology has been enjoying a resurgence of popularity in recent decades. The Sydney Anglican Diocese, often critical of other more 'liberal' Anglican dioceses in other parts of the world, is unashamedly Calvinistic—hence the answer to Anthony's question.

Calvinism takes the doctrine of Christ's atonement to new heights-or depths, depending on your perspective. In order to exalt the absolute 'sovereignty' of God (his will is absolute in all things), the doctrine of salvation is given a stricter, harsher, more conservative tone. Not only does Christ's atoning death provide the *only* means of salvation, it is *only* effective for the elect. God pre-determined, even before the creation of the world, the exact number and identity of those who would be saved—he didn't leave that to chance—and the exact number of those who would not be saved. This is the doctrine of *predestination*. Salvation is wholly a matter of God's will and grace, rather than of man's will or choice. This implies, as Calvinism teaches, that Christ's atonement was of a 'limited' nature, not in terms of its efficacy, but in terms of the number of souls Christ died for. He died only for the elect. If Judaism found Paul incomprehensible, it certainly finds Calvin doubly so.

Calvinism adheres to the most pessimistic view of human nature. As a result of the 'Fall', all humankind is hopelessly lost in sin, depraved in every aspect of their being. No one is capable of turning to God and seeking his salvation. God's grace must make the heart of the individual willing to seek him. This saving grace, results in the benefits of Christ's death being attributed to the seeker who is now able to trust in and believe in Christ. The fact that millions of others do not seek God is the natural result of their 'fallen' sinful nature. They are spiritually dead and when they die, they will be eternally lost. Those who are saved by God's electing will, can never lose their salvation. God guarantees the outcome of their faith in him. All of this is summarized in the acronym TULIP—Total Depravity, Unconditional Election, Limited Atonement, Irresistible Grace and Perseverance of the believer.

When I was ordained a Presbyterian minister of the 'Word and Sacraments', I swore to uphold the teachings of the Westminster Confession of Faith, a document produced in the Seventeenth century, one hundred years after Calvin's death. Chapter Three on 'God's Eternal Decrees' outlines this theology of salvation. At the beginning of my ministry I was a passionate Calvinist, but half-way through I had become far more liberal in my views of salvation. The contents of this confession of faith which constitutes the doctrine of all Reformed churches, now fills me with a sense of dismay and even revulsion. I find it hard to believe that I once thought of God in the way he is portrayed in the Confession.

> In order to manifest His glory God has ordered that some men and angels should be predestined to everlasting life and that others should be foreordained to everlasting death. This predestination and

foreordination of angels and men is precise and unchangeable. The number and identity of angels and men in each group is certain, definite and unalterable ... . God has chosen in Christ those of mankind who are predestined to life and everlasting glory. He has done this solely out of His own mercy and love and completely to the praise of His wonderful grace. This choice was completely independent of His foreknowledge of how His created beings would be or act. Neither their faith nor good works had any part in influencing His selection.

Only the elect and no others, are redeemed by Christ, effectually called, justified, adopted, sanctified and saved. ... For the glory of his sovereign power over his creatures, it pleased God not to call the rest of mankind and ordain them to dishonour and wrath for their sin, to the praise of His glorious justice.[2]

Even allowing for the peculiar expression of seventeenth-century English divines, this document paints a disturbing, horrific picture of the God millions of Christians believe in. We are told by defenders of this doctrine, that it is wrong and ignorant to suggest that God is acting arbitrarily like a celestial tyrant and that such decrees defy any human sense of justice or mercy. Incredibly the Confession tells us that such sovereign actions on God's part 'manifest His *glory*,' that he has done this 'out of His own *mercy* and *love*', and that this is an expression of his 'wonderful grace'. What a radical reappraisal of glory, mercy, love and grace is required in order to swallow these bitter pills. Can words have any meaning if these do?

How can such attributes be matched to such unprecedented and irrational cruelty? No wonder Methodists, representing another later branch of the Reformation, called Calvin's God their Devil! To state that 'It *pleased* God' to pre-determine that hundreds of millions if not billions of human beings would, after a brief sojourn on Earth, be consigned to everlasting damnation, is enough to render even the most tolerant student of religion speechless. I regard the Westminster Confession of Faith as one of the best arguments for atheism. If you are going to invent or imagine a god, you can't do worse than this.

When you think of the hundreds of millions consigned to eternal damnation, even before they were born, the question naturally arises, what did they do to deserve such a dreadful fate? The answer as we have already seen, lies in the doctrine of the 'Fall'. Whatever Adam did in Eden, whatever imperfect nature he passed on to all humankind, it is so serious, so deserving of God's wrath and judgment, that everyone deserves damnation—everyone! So Calvinists say we should praise God's 'wonderful grace' because, though not obliged to save any such undeserving creatures, he has chosen to extend his mercy and saving grace to some.

Isn't that wonderful! It is incredible to think that sane, ordinary, otherwise intelligent people believe such things about salvation and about God! Could there be any greater proof of the absurdity and false nature of a very significant portion of Christianity than this? Such Christians can talk about the love and mercy of God all they like, but this God must surely be the most inexplicable and monstrous creation of the human imagination. He would, in fact, fit more comfortably among the flora and fauna of Terry Pratchett's *Discworld* than between the pages of the Bible. I should add that since the Seventeenth century, many Christians of the Reformed faith have moved away from their original harsh Calvinist legacy.

The Church of Scotland, in which my infant baptism occurred, as well as the Church of England whose 'Thirty-Nine Articles' are a basically Reformed/Calvinist theology, have become very much more liberal in their outlook, though there are always pockets of 'reformers' within both denominations who want their churches to be true to their heritage. Many Presbyterians and Anglicans or Episcopalians as they are known in the United States, would not consider themselves Calvinists or want to defend the 'Five Points of Calvinism' (Tulip) with any enthusiasm. In my last years as a Presbyterian minister, prior to a period ministering in Baptist churches, I knew a number of elders on the Kirk Session of the congregation who had never really read the Westminster Confession of Faith. In some Presbyterian churches in Sydney and elsewhere, it would be mandatory that elders read, understood and promoted the Confession. In others it would be regarded as an antiquated distraction.

One indication of the strength of Calvinism today is its influence in the United States. In a January, 2014 report, the *New York Times* noted that Evangelicalism (conservative Protestantism) is in the midst of a Calvinist revival. It drew attention to some of the preachers and scholars who teach Calvin's theology—Mark Driscoll (now fallen somewhat out of favor), John Piper and Tim Keller. They are megachurch pastors and best-selling authors in the Christian market. During the Nineteenth century, Protestantism moved toward the non-Calvinist belief that humans must consent to their own salvation—a more positive and optimistic belief, commonly labeled Arminianism. Billy Graham for example based his preaching and appeals for a response, for a 'decision for Christ' on the basis of this more optimistic view of human ability and responsibility. Graham is not a Calvinist.

What is interesting about this article is that the Calvinist or neo-Calvinist revival is having an impact on the very demographic group the church is losing—young people, something we have known for some time. Much as I have expressed wonderment about why anyone would want to believe such a harsh theology, the sobering fact is that they are actually lining up to do so!

> Mark Dever's Capital Hill Baptist Church in Washington ... has grown from 130 members to 1,000, with an average age of 30. And while Mr. Dever tends not to mention Calvin in his sermons, his educated audience, many of whom work in politics, knows and likes what it is hearing ... 'I think it is apparent in his teaching,' said Sarah Rotman, 34, who works for the World Bank. 'The real focus on Scripture, and that all the answers we seek in this life can be found in the word of God. In a lot of his preaching, he does really talk about our sinfulness and our need of the Saviour.'[3]

One of the reasons the article cites for the interest of young people in Calvinism, is their dissatisfaction with the prevailing pop-theology, 'prosperity gospel' preaching that makes people feel good and treats the Bible like a self-help book or guide to better business. Joel Osteen has been spectacularly successful preaching this kind of gospel. They want something of more substance and they want to hear more about Jesus. As Collin Hanson in his book, *Young, Restless, Reformed* pointed out, the twenty and thirty-somethings want more formal, historical, transcendent worship. They are being drawn to places where pastors and Christians are 'intelligent but overtly and unapologetically Christian and confessional (systematic theology) and theological and expositional (unpacking the meaning of Scripture). And it's like the moth to a flame.'[4]

A prominent example of the Calvinist influence in America is Richard Albert (Al) Mohler. He is a theologian and ninth president of the Southern Baptist Theological Seminary in Lousiville, Kentucky—the largest seminary in the USA. He also hosts a nationwide radio show which seeks to engage contemporary culture with Christian belief. Mohler has succeeded in transforming SBTS into 'ground-zero' for Calvinism in America.

The seminary is training the ministers who will carry the banner for Calvinism in hundreds of churches. Mohler is a Calvinist who believes that Jesus is the only way for people to attain salvation and have a relationship with God the father. Salvation cannot be earned, but is a free gift given by God only to the elect. He has publicly stated that this excludes Judaism, Islam—and Catholicism! He believes that any other 'ism' that prevents people from coming to faith in Jesus Christ, is a demonstration of satanic power. During a 2000 television interview on *Larry King Live,* Mohler said of Catholicism: 'As an evangelical, I believe that the Roman Catholic Church is a false church. It teaches a false gospel. And the Pope himself holds a false and unbiblical office.'[5]

Non-believers can only stand back and gasp at the *intolerance* of believers, particularly conservative Evangelical Christian believers. Here is a man, the president of one of the world's most influential theological seminaries, who does not believe that the Roman Catholic Church, the oldest, most numerous body of Christians in the world, is a legitimate or true Christian Church. Catholics too, along with Jews and Muslims are in need of 'saving.' He accuses Catholicism of preaching a 'false gospel' while promoting his own Calvinist gospel which declares not only that *only* the 'elect' can be saved, but that even *within* the world Christian community, the elect are overwhelmingly confined to Protestants.

So great has the Calvinist influence become in the Southern Baptist Convention (America's largest denomination Protestant group) that in 2004, that Convention formally withdrew from the Baptist World Alliance (BWA), an international fellowship of 231 conventions and unions in 121 countries and territories comprising 42 million members in 177,000 churches. The withdrawing Convention spokesmen cited 'a continual leftward drift' in the BWA (read more inclusive, tolerant and less socially conservative), finding it could not compromise its own theology and outlook with the more 'liberal' theology of Baptists. BWA general secretary Denton Lotz, brother-in-law of popular Bible teacher Anne Graham Lotz, Billy Graham's daughter, was mystified with this secessionist decision. 'We certainly are not liberal. We're all conservative evangelicals.'[6]

Paige Paterson, President of the Southern Baptist Convention at the time its delegates voted overwhelmingly to secede from the world body, accused the wider world body of betraying the Gospel. 'Nor is it possible for us to be any longer in affiliation with some of the denominations of the BWA who do not believe in the inerrancy and infallibility of Scripture and regularly call it into question.' There were additional social issues that Paterson accused the BWA of being too 'liberal' on.

Let's take stock of this and attempt to grapple with what these Evangelical-Reformed Christians are trying to tell us. Jesus is the only way to salvation, so only Christianity is the true religion. But Catholics are not real or true Christians, so they need saving along with members of all other world religions. Then again, Jesus died only for the 'elect', so only those pre-destined or chosen by God to be saved, will be saved. And even *within* those we might have assumed are the 'elect'—conservative Evangelical Protestants—there are those we need to withdraw from because of their unfaithfulness to Scripture and betrayal of the Gospel. How many people then, do we imagine will actually make it to Heaven? Not many apparently.

Irony upon irony. Protestants break with Catholics in the Sixteenth-century Reformation, mainly over differing views as to how humans receive salvation. Five hundred years later—though there have been many similar incidents before—the Southern Baptist Convention which has become far more Calvinist, splits away from its parent-body, mainly over how Scripture should be interpreted and understood—salvation again being an issue. Meanwhile, the three-thousand year old Jewish community that has always insisted that *how you live* rather than what you *believe*, is more important for 'salvation', tells us that it is Christianity that misinterprets the Scriptures.

Let's imagine how it might have sounded if Rabbi Stuart Federow, author of *Judaism and Christianity: A Contrast,* had addressed the Southern Baptist Convention in 2004 and, after explaining all the misinterpretations of the Bible Christians are guilty of, had said:

> Christianity is not in agreement with, but is antithetical to, the clear, simple, consistent meaning of the Hebrew Scriptures ... If the Bible is to be believed, if it is to be accepted as authoritative, then the beliefs of Christianity are contrary to what the Bible clearly, simply, and consistently states ... if the Christian understanding, however they reach their understanding, is contrary to the Bible, then their beliefs are simply unbiblical and must be rejected by all those who believe in the authority of the Bible.[7]

Of course there would have been a resounding and thunderous denunciation of such a statement. Had Federow then announced that the Jewish World Alliance was instigating steps to reclaim the 'Old' Testament for Judaism's exclusive use and compel Christian publishers to only publish the New Testament, he probably would have been in need of a police escort from the premises.

As debate and criticism about the doctrine of atonement and salvation has continued to grow in the last few decades, some Evangelical scholars have attempted to encourage consensus and reconciliation of differing views. During the first decade of the Twenty-first century, the nature and effects of Christ's atoning death became the subject of considerable debate and controversy. Strange isn't it, how this whole doctrine of atonement/salvation continues to be so difficult to explain. Leading Christian scholars published books expressing different views and numerous addresses were presented at symposiums in the United Kingdom and North America. Influential and well-published theologians like the former Anglican Bishop of Durham, Tom Wright, promoted what was called the 'new perspective' on Paul, seeking to clarify the essential nature of the 'Gospel.'

In a telling statement evidencing the continuing inability of the Christian Church to fully understand its own doctrine of salvation, Wright says in his conclusion: 'What comes out of the text itself (Scriptures) is the fact, and the achievement, of Jesus Christ himself. In ways that the Western tradition, Catholic and Protestant, Lutheran and Calvinist—yes, and Anglican too!—has often failed to recognize, scripture forms a massive and powerful story whose climax is the coming into the world of the unique son of the one creator God, and above all, his death for sins and his bodily resurrection from the dead'.[8]

The British Evangelical theologian Ian Howard Marshall (1934–2015) was Professor Emeritus of New Testament Exegesis and Honorary Research Professor at the University of Aberdeen, Scotland. He was formerly the chair of the Tyndale Fellowship for Biblical and Theological Research as well as president of the British New Testament Society and chair of the Fellowship of European Evangelical Theologians. He is an Evangelical Methodist and is the author of numerous publications, including the 2005 Gold Medallion Book Award winner, *New Testament Theology*. His book, *Aspects of the Atonement*, published in 2007, sought to make sense of this 'intense debate and criticism' and clarify the meaning of the atonement. Supporters of Marshall like theologian Henri Blocher saw Marshall's book as an effective counter to 'books of dubious scientific value (which) have recently clouded the vital issue of the atonement, *leaving many readers confused*.'[9] (emphasis mine). When you have gone down the Christian rabbit hole, confusion is inevitable.

Marshall's primary objective in writing his book was his concern that among the theologians 'rejecting the concept of penal substitution' (Christ took our punishment and died in our place on the cross) was the fact that some of them are evangelical, 'so their questioning has caused something of a furore among those colleagues who regard penal substitution as an essential element in Christian doctrine.'[10] Marshall argues for a doctrine he feels is 'well-founded in Scripture' and that can be defended against the objections brought against it.

Protestants broke with Roman Catholicism in the Sixteenth century Reformation because they believed that Scripture and not the Church (which had defined how Scripture ought to be interpreted for a thousand years) should govern and define Christian belief. Since then, Scripture has spectacularly failed to keep Protestants from disputing with one another over the meaning of Scripture. Marshall wanted to defend views he thought were clearly taught in Scripture against those who interpreted those views differently.

In the previous chapter I analysed John Stott's writings on *The Cross of Christ*. Stott wrote another book in tandem with the Rev. David L. Edwards, Provost of Southwark and former editor of SCM Press. The book is called

Essentials: A liberal-evangelical dialogue (1988). Stott defends traditional evangelical doctrine against the objections of a liberal Anglican scholar like Edwards. Unexpectedly the book caused an uproar in evangelical circles because of a statement Stott made at the end in which he suggested that those judged unworthy of heaven are not punished eternally, but 'annihilated'. They cease to exist. 'Both the language of destruction and the imagery of fire seem to point to annihilation'[11]

So vehement were attacks on Stott, that some condemned him as no longer being Evangelical! This is the man who for decades, defined and defended Evangelicalism, but because he took a contrary view on this one issue, he was severely criticized. As Scott McKnight observed, so severe were the attacks on Stott that, 'because of the way he was treated, in spite of impeccably careful exegesis (of Scripture), many simply chose to keep their embrace of annihilationism under wraps'. McKnight went on to say that despite such opposition a growing number of Evangelical theologians were publicly advocating this revised view and publishing views similar to those of Stott.

Stott himself provided us with a glimpse into the Evangelical Christian mind when he called the Christian confidence and insistence over the fate of the wicked suffering eternally, a 'horrible sickness of mind or spirit'. He said that he himself found the view of eternal suffering in Hell, 'intolerable' and that he could not 'understand how people can live with it without either cauterizing their feelings or cracking under the strain'. McKnight agrees with Stott that 'there is an incommensurate justice to punish temporal sin eternally.'[12]

More gentle opposition to the views of Stott came from leading Reformed theologian J.I. Packer who considered advocates of annihilationism or 'conditional mortality' like Stott and Philip Edgcumbe Hughes to be in error. Gentle or harsh, the divisions in the Christian world over this and other doctrines remains. Wayne Grudem in his *Systematic Theology*, insists that 'we cannot accept as faithful to Scripture the doctrine of annihilationism ... such an idea is not explicitly affirmed in any passages of Scripture.'[13] John Stott, Philip Hughes, F.F. Bruce and I. Howard Marshall beg to differ. No wonder people looking at Christianity from the outside are confused.

Back to Marshall. Let's see if he can make the matter any clearer for us. For Evangelicals like Marshall there may not be total agreement about the nature of Hell, but there is far greater agreement about the nature of Christ's atoning death. Salvation, Marshall contends, is necessary because 'God is angered by the misdeeds of his creatures.'[14] Those misdeeds have broken the relationship between God and humankind. 'In the last analysis, 'the wages of sin is death.'[15] He recognizes that there is no element of reform or restitution in God's final condemnation of the wicked. Because of that, he sees no point in never-ending punishment, but favours an interpretation of Scripture that appears to support 'final, irreversible destruction.'[16]

He quotes P.T. Forsyth, whom he regards as the classical theologian who has done most to present a doctrine of atonement that takes God's holiness fully into account: 'There is a penalty and curse for sin; and Christ consented to enter that region ... It is impossible for us to say that God was angry with Christ; but still Christ entered the wrath of God ... You can therefore say that although Christ was not punished by God, He bore God's penalty upon sin.'[17] Notice the carefully qualified explanations that again remind us that we are tumbling down a rabbit's hole when it comes to talking about Christian salvation. When Forsyth insists that Christ was not punished by God, but that he 'entered the wrath of God', then we are indeed, entering the unknown, the disorientating or the mentally deranging; a period of chaos and confusion. It is a clear example of theologically having your cake and eating it too.

Salvation is essentially about a sacrifice offered for sin. Marshall re-states this basic assumption. 'Sacrifice is costly, and it involves the death of a victim ... who would otherwise have been spared. In his sacrificial death we see God, in the Son, bearing the consequences of our sin so that we do not have to bear them.'[18] This is the basic message of Christian evangelism and it reminds us that we should be bolder in not allowing such incomprehensible 'god-talk' to go unchallenged.

We might simply ask what a statement like this means and raise the question of *who* is actually being sacrificed for our sins. Theologians are usually found chasing their tails when it comes to answering this difficult question. I mentioned previously that Christianity's official, orthodox teaching is that Jesus, as God's Son dies for our sins, and that it is heresy to say that God (the father) died for our sins. But having once compromised their Jewish inheritance of monotheism—belief in one God—Christians are stuck with their idea of the Holy Trinity, an idea that renders the Cross of Christ enigmatic to say the least.

Marshall explains that talk of Jesus' intercession between God and humankind 'must be understood as a figure of speech from human relationships that must not be pressed too far to imply that the Father's mind is different from that of the Son or the Spirit'. The term 'intercession' he says, is a 'condescension to human beings who might think of God as other than Jesus whom they know as the friend of sinners'. In other words, Marshall is trying to maintain the doctrine of the Trinity—'three persons' in one God—while affirming, impossibly, that there is still only *one* God. His conclusion is therefore inevitable.

> There is an indissoluble unity between Father, Son and Holy Spirit in the work of redemption. The recognition that it is God the Son, that is to say quite simply God, who suffers and dies on the cross, settles the question finally. This is God himself bearing the consequences of our sin, not the abuse of some cosmic child'.[19]

He has already said that Christ was not punished by God, but he bore the penalty for sin. Now he adds that God 'himself' dies on the cross. Does God die or is it Christ who dies? Even Marshall can't seem to give a satisfactory answer. He immediately appreciates that the objective onlooker, including unbelievers who find this to be extraordinary and mystifying, naturally wonder what is going on while Christ is dying. Where is the Father? Can God die? What happens to the universe when God dies? Why does Jesus feel forsaken on the cross? Why does he cry out to God as if God is someone 'other' than himself? Marshall admits:

> Indeed, there are mysteries here that we cannot fathom. God the Father is there at the cross, self-sacrificially giving his Son to be one with humanity and die for its sins, and somehow there is a separation as the Son ... bears their sins. Paradoxically God is both present and absent. The Bible shows Jesus not just as a representative, substitutionary man bearing the sins of the world, but as God, God the Son, God in Christ, taking on himself the sin of the world and its consequences, and enduring them in himself ... 'Tis mystery all, the immortal dies'. Faith cries out, Tis he, my God, who suffers there!' (Charles Wesley).[20]

Again he insists that 'the death is the death of God himself, since the Son is one with the Father, and we are correct to see God dying on the cross, as Charles Wesley's hymns clearly teach'. Judaism, after two thousand years of being brow-beaten by this new gospel which claims to have superseded it, continues to shake its collective head. Unbelievers simply feel reinforced in their unbelief. Marshall knows 'that the concept of God the Son suffering and dying is paradoxical and incomprehensible, and we have to recognize that fact, but that is what Scripture says'.[21] Here is the circular argument again. The sense of the doctrine is paradoxical and incomprehensible, but because it is taught in the New Testament, we have to accept it. Why? Why not question the New Testament?

To make it more confusing, in the very next chapter, Marshall states that 'the death of Jesus is the death of the Son of God, and not the death of the Father'.[22] I can well recall using all these familiar phrases and explanations in my own teaching and preaching and sometimes wondering whether people really understood what I was saying or, worse still, really believed it. Most of the time they just accepted it because somewhere at the back of their minds they have convinced themselves that true 'faith' must always be incomprehensible and that the authority of Scripture, God' Word, is not to be questioned. It is not a rational or entirely comfortable way to live. One member of the Trinity dies, but not the others. This is supposed to make sense if we remember that one member of the Trinity became 'incarnate', that is, was born into the world as a human being, thus making it possible for him to die.

If God the father and Jesus the Son are really the 'one' God, then it is hard to avoid the conclusion that this one God has somehow created an extension of himself and projected it into the world of human beings. That of course is considered to be a crude and inadequate, albeit sensible way, of understanding the Trinity. Christianity rejects it because it insists that the Son and the Holy Spirit, the two other 'personages' of the Holy trinity are 'co-equal' 'co-eternal' with God. Jesus or God the Son did not start to exist when he was born into the world, he has existed eternally. He is not merely another 'mode' or manifestation of God, he *is* God. This is why Marshall has to insist that God didn't die, but also that God *did* die. Confused? I don't blame you.

By making mystery and incomprehensibility the unique mark of its doctrine of salvation, Christianity alone, of all the world's religions, struggles with its attitude towards the 'others', those who follow other religious paths. The more conservative Christian churches don't 'struggle' at all. For them, Christ is the only Saviour and everyone outside of the salvation he offers is eternally condemned and lost. It's unfortunate, but there it is. For many other Christians this is problematic to say the least.

Marshall does not actually develop this question at any length, but in the conclusion to his book he does say that, 'As Christians, we have a duty to proclaim our gospel and our ethic as the right and best way for humanity, but this does not mean that we refuse to recognize the value of other approaches that have some positive effect.'[23] This is a common Evangelical response.

You admit that there is some value and goodness, even truth, in the other religions, but in the end, they are not true *enough* to save anyone.

The doctrine of atonement or salvation is not a doctrine that can easily be garnered from the teachings of Jesus or from the four gospels. The doctrine depends so much on the teachings of the apostle Paul, that it would be no exaggeration to propose that we rename Christians, *Paulians.* E.P. Sanders in one analysis of Paul's teachings, helpfully talks about 'the solution as preceding the problem'.[24] Traditionally, Sanders observes, theologians have always begun with the 'plight' of man to which Paul saw Christ as offering a 'solution.' This is 'as in Adam all die, so in Christ shall all be made alive' hypothesis. Sanders himself does not believe that moving from 'plight' to 'solution' gives as an accurate picture of Paul's thinking. He believes that Paul's thought ran from 'solution' to plight.' In other words, Paul *started* with Christ the Saviour and then justified his role as Saviour by talking about the need for a saviour.

> It appears that the conclusion that all the world—both Jew and Greek—equally stands in need of a saviour *springs from* the prior conviction that God had provided such a saviour. If he did so, it follows that such a saviour *must* have been needed, and then only consequently that all other possible ways of salvation are wrong. The point is made explicitly in Galatian 2:21: If righteousness could come through the law, Christ died in vain. The reasoning apparently is that Christ did not die in vain; he died and lived again 'that he might be Lord both of the dead and the living' (Romans 14:9).[25]

With this interpretation of Paul's mindset it is easy to understand why Judaism rejected Paul's reverse way of thinking. Judaism did not start with Christ as saviour or conclude that a saviour must be needed. Nothing in the 'Old' Testament hinted at such a thing. Jews were saved by God and expressed that salvation by living by God's law. But because Paul and subsequently Christianity started with the 'solution'—Christ the Saviour—it automatically became an exclusive religion, considering 'lost' all those outside of belief in Christ. This is why Sanders adds, in the next sentence, that 'If his (Christ's) death was *necessary* for man's salvation, it follows that salvation cannot come in any other way and consequently that all were, prior to the death and resurrection, in need of a saviour. There is no reason to think that Paul felt the need of a universal saviour prior to his conviction that Jesus was such'[26].

Paul's reasoning is similar to that of that much later figure in history, Joseph Smith, the founder of the Mormon Church. Smith claimed that God had appeared to him and given him instructions to 'restore' Christ's true church to the earth. Mormonism is synonymous with 'Restorationism' rather than reform. The whole rationale for the existence of this Nineteenth century American religious movement, is that 'true' Christianity had already been lost and had ceased to exist. Joseph Smith argued from the 'solution'—Mormonism is God's divine latter day work evidenced by the prophetic career of the Prophet Joseph Smith and the appearance of the Book of Mormon as a new scripture.

Mormonism provides the 'solution' to the obvious 'plight' of a world in need of 'true' Christianity. Sounds reasonable except that such a claim rested entirely on the assumption that there was no Christianity or salvation in the world, that there had been an 'apostasy' of the original church and that the world could now only be saved through the 'Restored Gospel' of Mormonism. Something new had appeared in the world and therefore there had to be a complete revision of the entire ecclesiastical narrative that had gone before it.

Likewise with Paul. Something new had appeared in the world—Jesus the Christ, the promised Messiah and saviour. Having accepted that premise, Paul had to rewrite the entire religious narrative that had gone before, namely Judaism. In order to justify the role of Christ he had to negate Judaism's role as the pointer to God. It is only when we stand back and reflect on Paul's thinking that we grasp how strange and forced it really is. Sanders describes Paul's 'logic'.

> In Christ, God has acted to save the world; therefore the world is in need of salvation; but God also gave the law; if Christ is given for salvation, it must follow that the law could not have been; is the law then against the purpose of God which has been revealed in Christ? No, it has the function of consigning everyone to sin *so that* everyone could be saved by God's grace in Christ.[27]

It is the same as Mormonism's apologists saying that the whole history of historic Christianity served the function of displaying the inevitable apostasy and consequent need for a restoration. Christians would say however, that the Christian Church didn't need 'restoring' because it hadn't ever been lost or disappeared. It may have needed reforming, an experience it often undertook, but it did not need to be re-started. The 'prophet of the restoration' was therefore unnecessary. As far as the Jews were concerned, God had certainly urged them to reform on many occasions, but had never suggested that his covenant with them would be terminated and that some other movement would replace it. That is a purely New Testament assertion. The covenant with Israel was 'eternal', therefore a 'new' covenant in Christian terms was unnecessary. Christ was unnecessary in his role as saviour. No wonder Hyam Maccoby called Paul, 'The Myth-Maker'.

Engaging with a Liberal Theologian - John Hick

'But since that state (of the 'Fall') never existed, would it not be better to abandon the concept of the Fall altogether? For if we believe that there never was a human fall from an original paradisical state, why risk confusing ourselves and others by speaking as if there were?

– John Hick

Liberal-minded Christians hearing the kind of things I am asserting about Christian beliefs, would probably object that I am being too selective and only criticising a conservative or fundamentalist approach to atonement and salvation. They make the accusation that we atheists and ex-believers do not give enough of a hearing to the mainstream or 'liberal' Christians scholars and theologians. Now that is partly true, but since most Christian evangelism and outreach comes from those who are more conservative in their theology—Billy Graham conducted great crusades not Bishop John Shelby Spong—the response of non-believers like myself is usually directed at the conservatives.

Christians who are aware of the books written by atheists or 'New Atheists' often accuse these writers of not engaging sufficiently with theologians or of being only superficially acquainted with theology. The implication is that if they were more engaged or acquainted with theologians of a 'broader' outlook, their arguments against religion would not be as persuasive. I hope that I have so far demonstrated that I *am* engaged sufficiently with Christian theology, but I want to go further in this chapter and respond to one particular liberal theologian, John Hick (1922–2012). This famously liberal philosopher and theologian is described on the official Hick website as follows:

> John Hick was an internationally read and discussed philosopher of religion and theologian. His many books have, between them, been translated into seventeen languages. More than twenty books have been published about his work in English, German, French, Chinese and Japanese.
>
> Hick had doctorates from Oxford (D.Phil) and Edinburgh (D.Litt), and honorary doctorates from Uppsala University, Glasgow University and most recently Birmingham University (DD). He was an emeritus professor of both Birmingham University UK and the Claremont Graduate University, California. He was a Fellow of the Institute for Advanced Research in Arts and Social Sciences, University of Birmingham UK, and a Vice-President of the British Society for the Philosophy of Religion and of the World Congress of Faiths. The story of his life is told in John Hick: An Autobiography (2002).[1]

Theologians like Hick, James D.G. Dunn, Hans Kung and Richard Holloway with their more liberal outlook, enabled me to maintain my commitment to the Christian Faith during my years of questioning and increasing doubt. The liberal Christian position has its appeals and serves to relieve a lot of the tensions and problems inherent in religious faith. The fact that it is far more nuanced and inclusive, open to the wider world of knowledge and discovery, means it can be a real refuge for anyone struggling with doubts or intellectual difficulties. But in the end, it does tend to contradict the basic premises of the 'revelation' it seeks to re-interpret or re-envision. It often reads and sounds nebulous, insubstantial and mystical. Its non-traditional understanding of God is only marginally more substantial than any thought of God allowed by an agnostic. While I found much comfort in the writings of liberal theologians because they always seemed more open and honest and intelligent, more willing to grapple with the problems, I knew that the end result of their efforts was less than satisfactory. It has been said that once you start pulling the threads out of religion's carefully crafted quilt of precedent and prejudice, the whole fabric might unravel. It did for me. A commitment to liberal theology was unsustainable.

Those who do *not* subscribe to religious faith need to be better acquainted with the writings of people like John Hick. In many ways they make more sense of religion because they are more open-minded, tolerant and reasonable, the very attributes which lead their more conservative brethren to regard them with suspicion and sometimes with contempt. It is easy to understand liberal frustration with anti-religious and anti-Christian writings that attack an interpretation of religion that does not represent their views. That is not how *we* see God, they say. That is not how *we* think of salvation. That is not what *we* think of the situation of non-Christians! And because even fewer Christians and members of the non-Christian public tend to read the works of the more academic, liberal theologians, preferring instead popular works of devotion and Christian teaching, the liberal voice is not sufficiently heard. When it is heard, particularly in the Church, it can sound unexpectedly refreshing, liberating, enlightening. But for most Evangelicals it sounds like a plain denial of God's inerrant word, a watering down of the strong, distinctive truths of the Gospel.

Though they certainly do not intend to challenge or shake real faith in the transcendent, liberal theologians are, in some ways, much closer to agnostics and atheists in their expressions than are to conservative, fundamentalist believers. This brief analysis of John Hick's *The Metaphor of God Incarnate: Christology in a Pluralistic Age* (Second edition, 2005), should make that clear. In fact throughout this book, Hick repeatedly uses phrases describing conservative Christian theology in the same way that I have in these chapters. And while I have been a little self-conscious and anxious about using terms which might sound intemperate or harsh, Christian theologians like Hick are not at all hesitant to call a spade a spade. He describes traditional and conservative Christian teachings as 'unbelievable', 'moral absurdity', 'totally implausible', 'morally grotesque', 'religious absurdity', 'highly implausible', 'morally repugnant'. No atheist could improve on that. As I re-read *The Metaphor of God Incarnate* I found myself agreeing with almost everything Hick wrote, though obviously coming to a slightly different overall conclusion.

What is it that theologians like Hick are telling us about 'the reconceptualization of Christian faith that is so badly needed'? Hick tells us that he is 'going to argue that in this narrower sense the idea of atonement is a mistake', and that his views reflect 'a widespread contemporary perception'.[2] By 'narrower' sense he means the view which I have been analysing in these chapters. That view is directly linked to the idea of the Fall and Original Sin and here Hick is in no doubt about the credibility of that doctrine.

> Today the idea of an actual fall resulting in a universal inherited depravity and guilt is totally unbelievable for educated Christians. Instead of the human race being descended from a single, specially created pair, we see the species as having evolved out of lower forms of life over an immensely long period of time. Instead of the earliest humans living in perfect communion with the God of Judaeo-Christian monotheism, we see them as probably having a primitive animistic outlook.[3]

Evangelicals typically equate 'educated' Christians with those who are willing to adopt dubious scientific 'theories' rather than the word of God. In North America, but also elsewhere, conservative Christians who still maintain an irrational prejudice against Darwin's theory of evolution through natural selection, refuse to accept what the overwhelming evidence of all the Earth sciences clearly demonstrates, namely the true origins of the human species. While many Christians struggle to find some compatibility between the worldview of science and that of the Biblical account of Genesis, theologians like Hick state plainly that science is fact, Genesis is myth.

> If out of piety towards the traditional language we wish to retain the term 'Fall', we can say that the earliest humans were, metaphorically speaking, already 'fallen' in the sense of being morally and spiritually imperfect. That is to say, they can be said to be as though they had fallen from an ideal state. *But since that state never existed* (emphasis mine), would it not be better to abandon the concept of the Fall altogether? For if we believe that there never was a human fall from an original paradisical state, why risk confusing ourselves and others by speaking as if there were?[4]

The idea of the 'Fall' is as dated and erroneous as was the pre-Copernican Mediaeval idea of a universe that revolved around the Earth. When in the Sixteenth century Copernicus formulated a new model of the universe that placed the Sun rather than the Earth at its centre, he was proposing precisely what Hick is proposing that we do with the idea of the Fall. Many Christians have made this adjustment, but even those who accept the evolutionary model for the origins of life, find themselves troubled by certain Scripture texts that uphold the teaching of the Fall.

In a previous chapter we discussed the apostle Paul's epistle to the Romans and his statement that 'death came through a human being (Adam) ... for as all die in Adam (original sin) so all will be made alive in Christ' (1 Corinthians 15: 21,22). This is not a text Evangelicals feel they can lightly dismiss. The authority of Paul is behind it. The credibility of the New Testament is behind it. The whole doctrine of the atonement and the need for the saving death of Christ is built on just such a text. Adam's sin created one reality, Christ's death creates another. But Hick is saying that Adam is a myth, that there is no reality behind the legend of the 'Fall' and so why should we go on talking about it as if it is reality?

He makes it clear that it is precisely this faulty myth of the Fall and of original sin that has 'fed the traditional conceptions of atonement.'

Instead of going through some convoluted theological argument for how and when Adam and Eve may have fitted into our primate evolutionary past, Hick urges believers simply to accept the facts, labelling the traditional view 'a moral absurdity'.

> We cannot be guilty in the sight of God for having been born, within God's providence, as animals biologically programmed for self-protection and survival within a tough environment. And even if we discount our modern awareness of the continuity between *homo sapiens* and the rest of animal life, the moral principle behind the traditional doctrine is still totally unacceptable. Although evidently believable in the age in which it was propounded, the idea of a universal inherited guilt was losing plausibility by the end of the eighteenth century and had entirely lost it, for many, by the end of the nineteenth.[5]

One of my own discoveries in the torturous journey from faith to humanism, was what I call the 'antiquity of doubt', the realisation that earnest seekers and independent thinkers had been finding problems in the Bible for centuries. Criticisms of traditional views did not suddenly flare into existence with the occasional essay of some radical theologian. They certainly weren't first aired by popular atheist writers like Christopher Hitchens and Richard Dawkins, both of whom, often referred to critiques of Scripture centuries old. People have suspected and concluded for a very long time that traditional explanations of the faith were no longer persuasive or valid. Whether it was the French priest, Father Jean Meslier writing his *Testament* to atheism in 1729, or American founding father, Thomas Paine, publishing his *The Age of Reason* in 1794, the errors of Christianity have been exposed for some time. Which is why people like Hick say it is time that such archaic and misleading teachings should be abandoned.

Hick concluded that the theory of Christian salvation in its traditional form, is 'totally implausible'. I don't want Christians to necessarily become atheists, but before they make any further attempts to question my de-conversion or attempt to remind me of the 'truthfulness' of the Gospel,

I would like them to consider *why* their doctrine of atonement is 'implausible'. Perhaps they have already suspected, but feel that too much would be lost were they to seriously ask themselves that question.

> The idea that guilt can be removed from a wrongdoer by someone else being punished instead is morally grotesque. And if we put it in what might at first sight seem a more favourable light by suggesting that God punished Godself, in the person of God the Son, in order to be able justly to forgive sinners, we are still dealing with the religious absurdity of a moral law which God can and must satisfy by punishing the innocent in the place of the guilty.[6]

Hick goes on to quote St. Anselm of Canterbury (1033 – 1109) who had his own theory of the atonement, as saying that: 'it is a strange thing if God so delights in, or requires, the blood of the innocent, that he neither chooses, nor is able, to spare the guilty without the sacrifice of the innocent'. Strange indeed. Not too many Christian theologians I have read, are sufficiently well acquainted with Judaism to understand, as I have already insisted, that the Jewish worldview constitutes a serious critique of the inferior Christian worldview. Happily, Hick spends some time discussing the doctrine of repentance—what the Jews call *teshuvah*—and this leads him naturally to conclude that God *can* forgive us simply on the basis of our repentance. Why else should anything further be required? He writes in terms which any Jewish theologian would agree with.

> When we do wrong the kind of reparation required is that we do what we can to nullify or reverse the consequences of our action ... it is also appropriate to do something extra, which he (Swinburne) calls penance, by offering some additional service or gift to express the reality of our regret and sorrow at having wronged that other person.[7]

Because it is a more 'humanistic' faith, this description of repentance is pure Judaism. It is also, I might add, pure humanism, with its focus on the relationship between the person committing the offence (sin) and the person offended. Where Hick takes issue with the more traditional theologian Swinburne, is where Swinburne insists that this process of repentance and reparation needs to be carried over into our relationship with God. By contrast, Hick suggests that 'when we have offered reparation plus penance to the human beings whom we have injured, there is no further reparation-plus-penance to be made solely for God's benefit.' He adds, 'in doing all we can to repair matters with our wronged neighbour we are doing what genuine repentance requires'.[8]

This is a crucial point because if what Hick is saying is true, then what need *is* there for some further action on our part that 'benefits God'? Why must God's wounded honour, holiness and sense of justice be placated or provided for through some kind of atoning sacrifice? 'God cannot be benefited, and thus recompensed and atoned to, by any human acts in addition to those that benefit God's creation.' It is therefore not appropriate to depict Christ's death as 'an atoning sacrifice that benefits God and so enables God to forgive humanity'.[9]

Arguing for the sufficiency of repentance in itself as an act leading to forgiveness, is a significant statement for a Christian theologian to make. The point about there being no need for an additional element to the process which somehow benefits or satisfies God is a fundamental principle of Judaism. 'According to Judaism, *God Himself* cannot forgive us for our sins against another person. Only the person or persons whom we have hurt can forgive us'.[10] Prager and Tselushin remind us that God forgives only those sins committed against him alone. On the annual Day of Atonement, the Jewish equivalent of Christian Easter, the community rituals and liturgy atone for sins against God, not for sins against other people. Those must have been dealt with through reconciliation in the days before Yom Kippur.

On December 15, 1997, an article appeared in the *Wall Street Journal*, (and later in the *Reader's Digest* magazine in May 1998) under the title, *When Forgiveness is a Sin* by Dennis Prager. The article must have come as a surprise to many Christians not accustomed to thinking of forgiveness in the way Prager explained it. It told the story of three teenage girls shot dead in December of 1997 by a fellow student at an American high school. Some well-meaning classmates immediately hung up a sign announcing, 'We forgive you, Mike!'. Mike was Michael Carneal, the 14 year-old killer. Rabbi Prager wrote that many Christians subscribe to the view that they should forgive everyone who commits evil against anyone. Congregations are often admonished to be willing to forgive someone who has committed a public crime or even murdered Christian missionaries. Prager applauds the great moral influence for good that Christianity often exhibits, but on this occasion he wrote, 'I am appalled and frightened by this feel-good doctrine of automatic forgiveness'. He went on to outline the Jewish view.

> This doctrine advances the amoral notion that no matter how much you hurt others, your fellow citizens will forgive you. It destroys Christianity's central moral tenets about forgiveness. Even by God, forgiveness requires repentance, and *it can be given only by the one sinned against* (emphasis mine).

Prager referred to Jesus' teaching on forgiveness in relation to people who sin against you—'if your brother sins against *you* ...'. (Luke 17:3-4). He then illustrated his point.

> These days one often hears that 'It is the Christian's duty to forgive, just as Jesus forgave those who crucified him.' Of course, Jesus asked God to forgive those who crucified him. But Jesus never asked God to forgive those who had crucified thousands of other innocent people. Presumably he recognised that no one has the right to forgive evil done to others ... only those who are sinned against have that right ... Another defence offered for the student's response is that doing so is psychologically healthy. It brings 'closure'. This is therapy masquerading as idealism: 'I forgive because I want to feel better.'[11]

Hick is essentially promoting the Jewish view of repentance as being in itself sufficient. Prager and Telushkin explain it more fully.

> If a Jew does violate God's laws, Jewish law enables him or her to return to God and right action through repentance—in Hebrew, teshuvah, from

the word for 'return'. Teshuvah consists of three steps: the sinner must recognise his sin, feel sincere remorse at having sinned, and resolve to return to fulfilling the law. There was also a fourth step during the time of the Temple—the bringing of a sacrifice—but since the destruction of the Temple, this step has been unnecessary, *a fact long foreseen by the Bible.* In the words of the Prophet Hosea (14:1-3), prophesying of a time when the Temple would no longer be standing, 'turn to the Lord, say to him, forgive all iniquity and receive us graciously, *so we will offer the prayers of our lips instead of calves.*' Hosea's statement is paralleled by Proverbs 21:3, 'To do righteousness and justice, is more acceptable to God than sacrifices,' and by the book of Jonah, which recounts that when the people of Nineveh repented, their sins were forgiven by God despite the fact that they brought no sin-offering.[12]

As we read these different approaches to the issues of forgiveness, atonement and salvation, we cannot help but note the far more realistic Jewish perspective on these things. The reason why Christians generally avoid Hick's conclusion is that they are already committed to Christ as Saviour, so that any scheme of salvation which excludes him or renders him superfluous, is not acceptable. After having explained how repentance and forgiveness is a process between people and not necessarily one which involves some additional requirement towards God, Hick says that insisting God must be satisfied in some way is a 'category mistake in which God is treated as another individual within the same moral community as ourselves.' Hick rejects the Christian idea that Christ's sinless and righteous perfection is attributed to sinful humans once they trust in him as Saviour, a transaction that Christians subscribe to without much questioning as to whether it makes sense.

> How would one single, perfect human life, namely that of Jesus, count as all human beings having led perfect lives? Swinburne's answer at this point is that God was free to accept whatever God wished as an atonement for human sin. God could have chosen to accept some angel's act for this purpose. This is a deeply damaging admission, rendering it truly extraordinary that God should require the agonizing death of God's Son. For on Swinburne's view there was no necessity for the cross ... according to him it was entirely within God's free choice to establish the conditions

for human salvation. But in that case God's insistence on the blood, sweat, pain and anguish involved in the crucifixion of God's innocent Son now seems even to cast doubt on the moral character of God.[13]

If there was 'no necessity for the cross', then why did Christ die? Most Christians will argue backwards. The fact of Christ's death requires an explanation. Since those early Christians broke with Judaism and its take on salvation, and since those who become Christians today, accept Christ as their saviour, the meaning of his death must of necessity, be profound, spiritually significant and unique. It can't simply have been the culmination of tragic circumstances. Hick by contrast, does not argue backwards like that. He moves from one rational position to the next, willing to accept the implications of each step along the way. If repentance is sufficient in itself for forgiveness, then the cross is not inevitable, not necessary. He reminds us that 'there is no consensus among New Testament scholars as to how Jesus understood his own death', and then proceeds to reflect on that very question. To what extent did Jesus think of his impending death as having religious significance?

E.P. Sanders in his scholarly works on Judaism and Christianity suggests that 'there are general objections to the whole line of thought that has Jesus intending to die for others, rather than just accepting his death and trusting that God would redeem the situation and vindicate him'.[14] Hick agrees with this more minimalist interpretation. He thinks that even if Jesus did think of his death as some kind of sacrifice to God, such a sacrifice 'could only occur within the context of Jesus' apocalyptic expectation', meaning that he both preached and expected the imminent arrival of the kingdom of God which would usher in the new age and believed his death might be the trigger for that cosmic event. Beyond that, Hick states the obvious reality that Christianity has always been determined to ignore.

> Jesus' expectation, confidently taken up by the early church, was not fulfilled, and had faded out of the Christian consciousness before the end of the first century. The identification of Jesus as the eschatological

prophet inaugurating God's kingdom went with it, being progressively superseded by his exaltation to a divine status. This in turn made possible the various atonement theories which presuppose his divinity, eventually seeing the cross as 'a full, perfect and sufficient sacrifice for the sins of the whole world'.[15]

The whole, interminable historical period between Christ's death and the present is evidence of the unfulfilled hope, the failed mission. But since we are no longer dealing with the 'real' Jesus of Nazareth, then the figure into which he has been transformed, God the Son, second person of a divine Trinity, can still be thought of as dwelling in the heavens awaiting his Father's signal to return. The tragic death which was absolute and final has been made into an atoning death in order for Christ to continue to have an influence over the human race, to make him *necessary* for the human race. The stark reality of his sense of God-forsakenness on the cross, is deliberately blunted by the later stories of resurrection.

By moving from a true understanding of repentance and forgiveness and depicting Christ's death as probably inevitable but not *necessary* for salvation, Hick opts for a God who 'freely forgives sinners who come in genuine penitence and a radically changed mind', as opposed to atonement theories which explain '*why* God could not freely forgive penitent sinners.' He considers theories of the atonement, particularly the one I have discussed at length in this book, to be 'unintelligible' and 'doubly morally questionable'.

Hick accepts the failure of Christ's mission in terms of the expected end to human history, while the Christian churches refuse to acknowledge that failure. They are less willing to admit that Jesus did not intend to found a continuing church, or a new religion separate from Judaism. They have inherited the new religion that evolved from the first century A.D., with the New Testament as its foundational document and evidence of its 'truth.' Ironically, Jesus, later made into the 'Christ' was *not* the founder of that new religion. Conservatives who criticise liberals like Hick, understand that if the liberal version of the doctrine of salvation is correct, Christianity is no longer the one way to God. Hick asks:

> Will Christians come to see Christianity as one among several authentic ways of conceiving, experiencing and responding to the transcendent; and will they come to see Jesus, in a way that coheres with this, as a man who was exceptionally open to the divine presence? ... I have argued that this doctrine (of the atonement) has been a mistake, carrying unacceptable ethical implications and being contrary to Jesus' own teaching.[16]

When the disciples of Jesus asked him to teach them to pray, he gave them what is allegedly the 'Lord's Prayer'. Even people of no faith can probably recite it. The fascinating thing about the Lord's Prayer is that it is a very Jewish prayer. It reflects a Jewish view of things rather than a Christian view. Nevertheless, the Church father, Tertullian (160–220 A.D.) described it as a summary of the Gospel. In a lecture that John Hick delivered in 2006, six years before his death, he summarized much of what I have tried to say in this chapter.

> Now in this prayer we are taught to speak directly to God as our Father in heaven. There is no question of a mediator, or of having to ask through or in the name of Jesus. And we are taught here that God forgives us our wrongdoings when we forgive those who wrong us. There is no question of an atoning sacrifice being necessary. And there is no reference to a divine Trinity.[17]

The Twilight of Atheism?

If God makes any difference in the world—and what would be the point of believing in any God that didn't make a difference to the world?—then we should be able to see indications of his existence when we observe the world we find ourselves in ... The theological line of argument is the attempt to reconcile the existence of God with the facts about our world that seem to suggest his absence

– Rebecca Goldstein

In 2004 Oxford academic and Anglican theologian Alister McGrath's book, *The Twilight of Atheism: The Rise and Fall of Disbelief in the Modern World*, was published. The *New York Times* called this 'Gripping ... impressive intellectual range.' No doubt McGrath has an intellectual range, he is, after all, an articulate historical theologian, but the 'impressive' part of his range is more evident in his works on Christian history and theology. It is not nearly so impressive when it comes to dealing with the topic of atheism. To be fair, he does seem to concentrate on the last few centuries, rather than Atheism's last two to three millennia, though he makes slight reference in Chapter 1, to 'The Dawn of the Golden Age of Atheism', mentioning criticisms of the Gods in Classical Greece. But he hardly does justice to that period and place.

How is it possible for example, that he missed Epicurus whose influence would extend to the Renaissance and the Enlightenment, a pivotal figure in any discussion about agnosticism or atheism? This would be like discussing the history of Christianity without mentioning St. Augustine. Thomas Jefferson, third president of the United States once said, 'I am an Epicurean' but since McGrath makes no mention of Jefferson either, his Christian readers will be left in the dark both about Epicureanism and the anti-religious thinking and writing of Jefferson.

McGrath does refer to Lucretius, another very significant figure, but in only one sentence, and again with no mention of the fact that Lucretius was the Roman instrument for preserving and promoting the philosophy of Epicurus. There is one sentence referring to Protagorus, but again, no mention of his teachings or influence. Why ignore sceptics and deists simply because they are sceptics and deists, when they are obviously atheists as far as the traditional God of the monotheistic faiths is concerned? The subtitle for this book makes it clear that McGrath is mainly talking about the 'Modern' World, but since he does include a chapter on Greece, he might as well have done it justice. He doesn't.

If we really are witnessing the 'Twilight of Atheism' as McGrath asserts, then there ought to be some acknowledgement that atheism also has its roots in cultures far beyond those of the West and in times long pre-dating the modern world. How for example can atheism be in its 'Twilight' when more than half a billion Buddhists in the modern world *don't* believe in God? What of the appeal of Buddhism, not to mention its smaller cousin Jainism? McGrath is either unaware or uninterested in the fact that atheism is very much a part of ancient Eastern tradition.

Since McGrath is writing in Britain, why not some passing reference to Charles Bradlaugh, member of parliament, political activist and famous or infamous English atheist of the 19th century? Bradlaugh was elected to parliament but denied his seat because of his professed atheism and his refusal to swear a religious oath. Only because of the intervention of former prime minister William Gladstone and the playwright George Bernard Shaw, was he finally allowed to take his seat. Bradlaugh of course, represents that long line of principled and courageous freethinkers who, through the centuries have suffered persecution, imprisonment and death for being unbelievers. This is probably why McGrath fails to mention them in building his case against atheism. As a result we hear from him no comment about Baruch Spinoza of Amsterdam or Giordano Bruno who was burnt at the stake in Rome. Even with his focus on the Modern world, he omits to mention that Nehru, the first prime-minister of India and confidante of Gandhi, was an atheist. I can understand that he might wish to paint atheism in the worst possible light, but such a highly selective approach means McGrath falls somewhat short of the 'enormous scholarship' that the former Archbishop of Canterbury, Rowan Williams attributed to this book.

As I said in my Introduction, Christian apologists often accuse unbelievers or secularists of not sufficiently engaging with the writings of serious Christian theologians, but Christians themselves are guilty of this oversight. Granted a lot of the works of influential humanists have been published since McGrath's *Twilight of Atheism* in 2004, but not all. Paul Kurtz's *The Transcendental Temptation* was first published in 1986, John Schellenberg's *Divine Hiddenness and Human Reason* in 1993 and Anthony Grayling's *What is Good? The Search for the Best Way to Live* in 2003, just to mention a few. One year before McGrath had his book published, Julian Baggini released his *Atheism: A Very Short Introduction* through Oxford University Press. Even a cursory glance at Baggini's succinct but comprehensive little text would have corrected some of McGrath's dubious assumptions about atheism.

Elsewhere in his book McGrath refers to the poet Shelley, dismissing as insignificant because it covers no new ground, a provocative essay penned by Shelley which most Christians would never have heard of—

The Necessity of Atheism. Shelley, he insists is simply drawing attention to something believers already know, namely, that 'the existence of God cannot be proved and is ultimately a matter of faith.' There's a telling admission. He says that Shelley's atheism 'proves somewhat problematic' suggesting that he may simply have wanted to shock a complacent establishment or 'assert the right to argue about ... the existence of God'.[1] This is a bit dismissive of Shelley's passion and personal convictions, not to mention the fact that he was expelled from Oxford because he would not retract his essay. McGrath finishes his discussion of Shelley by quoting Robert M. Ryan as pointing out that most radical poets returned to 'orthodoxy' in their later works. Really? Did Shelley? Is this final, misleading comment supposed to reassure us that we ought not to take Shelley seriously?

McGrath does acknowledge that 'the most fundamental criticisms directed against Christianity have to do with the moral character of its God ... that the Christian God seems to fall short in goodness and wisdom.' In this same, final paragraph he writes that: 'Atheism arises mainly through a profound sense that religious ideas and values are at least inferior to, and possibly irreconcilable with, the best moral standards and ideals of human culture.'[2] This would have been a good place for him to have *started* his book rather than ending it. Having read his book again, I can't see that he has addressed these 'fundamental criticisms' adequately at all.

He seems to understand why an atheistic culture reacts to the doctrine of 'eternal damnation' and religious teachings which appear to violate the 'most fundamental notions of decency and even-handedness', and insists that 'Christianity must provide answers—good answers—to such fair questions and never assume that it can recycle yesterday's answers to today's concerns'.[3] Good point, but *The Twilight of Atheism* fails to provide good answers to these fair questions. In the last several pages of the book McGrath, having admitted that old, traditional, church-state forms of Christianity are indeed worthy of criticism by atheists, finishes by suggesting that new forms of Christian community evidence the spiritual vitality of religion. Strangely the new form he is particularly inspired by is Pentecostalism. The world is not moving in a secular direction, he observes, but rather in a spiritual direction, Christianity experiencing new, resurgent impetus in the Pentecostal-Charismatic movement worldwide.

He reminds us of the 'massive Pentecostal expansion', a powerful force against its 'secular rival (atheism)'. 'Pentecostalism seems to put its trust in the power of God to change people's lives' and is of immense importance for Christianity because of its 'sense of the immediacy of God's presence through the Holy Spirit'.[4] Pentecostalism can restore 'the felt loss of the presence of the divine in everyday life in the West.' It is astonishing that he should appeal to what looks increasingly like the most irrational and bizarre expression of Christianity in its long history. This is the Pentecostalism that is presently taking the African continent by storm, a continent that now boasts more Anglicans than there are in Europe.

African Christians, especially of the Pentecostal brand are mainly of the conservative tradition—anti-gay and anti-witchcraft. They are provoking a new age of dangerous superstition on that continent resulting in the persecution—often legally—of homosexuals as well as women and children accused of being possessed by demons. The Salem Witch Trials, now centuries old, have returned with a vengeance to Pentecostal Christian Africa. The majority of Christians now live in the southern hemisphere and not the European and American north. The future of the religion lies mainly with them in Africa and Asia.

McGrath believes that only religion offers humanity a better future. As far as he is concerned, 'it is *this* form of Protestantism that may be expected to resist erosion by atheism.'[5] If that future is going to be defined by the growing influence of conservative, Pentecostal Christians, then we have good reason to be concerned. Carl Sagan's plea for science as a 'candle in the dark' in the

'Demon-haunted world' seems more prescient than ever. And McGrath's assumption that religion, not atheism offers us a brighter future, begs the question, *which* religion. Of course he means Christianity in particular. What of Islam or Buddhism or Bah'ai or Unitarianism for that matter? If, for example, Buddhism proved to be the religion of the future, then we would be talking about the twilight of religion, of Christianity rather than atheism.

In the end, *The Twilight of Atheism* doesn't deal at all with atheism's critique of the Christian Gospel with all its troublesome, inconsistent and absurd dogmas. Instead, McGrath appears to restrict his response to atheism by focusing on the sins of institutional religion and by highlighting the historic instances of atheistic totalitarian regimes whose own dogmatic assertions violated humanism's fundamental principles as much as religion does. It would be interesting to see McGrath produce a revised edition of his book, a decade after this first edition. It might better engage with current atheist and humanist writers. I would suggest he include A.C. Grayling's *Towards the Light*, Greg Epstein's *Good without God: What a Billion Nonreligious People Do Believe* and Kenan Malik's *The Quest for a Moral Compass: A Global History of Ethics*. He would certainly have to engage with the writings of Paul Kurtz, Victor Stenger, Kai Nielsen, Robert Wright, Phil Zuckerman and John W. Loftus. For 'light' reading he might find Rebecca Goldstein's *36 Arguments for the Existence of God—A Work of Fiction*, challenging and enlightening.

I want to conclude this chapter with a brief look at what McGrath says about the topic of salvation. He approaches the topic as a conservative Evangelical, one who has taught theology at Oxford University as well as historical and systematic theology at Wycliffe Hall, Oxford University. My comments are based on the Conclusion of his compendium on doctrine, *Studies in Doctrine: Understanding Doctrine, The Trinity, Jesus and Justification by Faith* (1997). McGrath is aware that the tide has turned against Christian belief in many ways. He asks how it might survive in the future, acknowledging that in the past, in Europe and North America alike, it 'has relied too much on a favourable cultural milieu for its survival, knowing that its existence was safeguarded by social patterns of behaviour.'[6] He is concerned with how the Faith will survive if social factors favouring church membership are reversed, a situation that has been occurring at a dramatic rate for a number of years now.

Since faith 'must be won, rather than assumed', evangelism, or the proclamation of Christ to the world, must, of necessity, be focused on the doctrine of 'justification'. Since this is a theological term little understood by the general public, I include a definition here: Justification, in Christian theology, is God's act of removing the guilt and penalty of sin while at the same time declaring a sinner righteous through Christ's atoning sacrifice. In Protestantism, righteousness from God is viewed as being credited to the sinner's account through faith alone, without works. McGrath believes that this is the article or central belief by which the church stands or falls.

> The Christian Church takes its stand against a disbelieving world on the basis of the firm and constant belief that God *acted* in the death and resurrection of Jesus Christ to achieve something that will remain of permanent significance to human beings, so long as they walk the face of this planet knowing that they must die. We are exposed for what we really are—sinners—and are offered the possibility of transformation as a free gift of God.[7]

As we have already seen in the chapters prior to this one, the world has good reason for being 'disbelieving' when it comes to this particular claim. McGrath insists that the saving relationship which God has established with humankind through the death and resurrection of Jesus 'constitutes the only basis for authentic human existence on the face of this earth.'[8] Only one particular religion or belief system is true, and that religion is Christianity. There is no authentic living or existence in this life, outside of a relationship with God through Jesus Christ. This is certainly not a liberal Christian view, but it is consistent with the basic claims of the New Testament.

Several times in speaking about the transforming power of God's salvation, McGrath underlines the claim that this is the 'free gift of God'. This is another way of speaking about 'grace', the kind of grace sung about in that famous hymn, 'Amazing grace!' This concept is based on Pauline texts such as those found in Ephesians 2:8,9 'For by grace you have been saved through faith, and this is not your own doing ; it is the gift of God—not the result of works, so that no one may boast'. For centuries Christians have argued about whether the 'gift' refers to *salvation* or the act of *faith* itself. Protestants, especially those of the Reformed (Calvinist) and Evangelical traditions have interpreted it to mean that faith itself is the gift of God. But to suggest that Catholicism does not have the same high view of grace as Protestantism because it encourages good works as well as faith, is to seriously misrepresent the Catholic position. The Catechism of the Catholic Church states clearly that:

> Faith is a gift of God, a supernatural virtue infused by him. 'Before this faith can be exercised, man must have the grace of God to move and assist him; he must have the interior helps of the Holy Spirit, who moves the heart and converts it to God, who opens the eyes of the mind and makes it easy for all to accept and believe the truth.[9]

Such a statement is certainly consistent with the teaching of the New Testament. It is the kind of statement which led the Catholic theologian Hans Kung to say decades ago, that there was substantially no difference between what Catholics were saying and Protestants were saying about the doctrine of Justification. Indeed there has already been a considerable rapprochement between the Catholic and Lutheran Churches on the basis of that conclusion.

Like Protestants, Catholics also believe that the act of faith is *a human act* as well and that the human will and assent is involved in the process of receiving the gift of salvation. This does not imply that the act of believing somehow warrants the gift of salvation. The problem for unbelievers looking at the subtleties of Christian theology is that no single church tradition has ever fully explained how faith and grace work. McGrath believes that 'there exist real differences between Protestants and Roman Catholics over the matter of justification'. This is remarkable. McGrath has already said that this is the doctrine on which the church 'stands or falls' and yet these 'real differences' still exist between Protestants and Catholics. He is critical of the fact that in the modern period, Christian denominations prefer to concentrate on their agreements rather than their historic disagreements. He believes the disagreements remain significant and blames the churches lack of discernment on this point as the result of their having been influenced by the 'rationalism of the Enlightenment.' I have made my choice with the rationalism of the Enlightenment, but then I am no longer a Christian.

By defending the doctrine of Justification in the way he does, McGrath is highlighting the very element of Christian salvation that we have already considered to be defective and irrational. He repeatedly refers to 'original sin', but never actually spells it out in the traditional literal terms of the book of Genesis. For him, salvation is all God's work.

> 'Nothing we can do can be said to be the basis or ground of our own justification. Even faith (emphasis mine) itself must be recognized as a divine gift and work within us. We cannot turn to God unless God turns to us first. The priority of God's redeeming will and action over our own actions in bringing about our salvation is expressed by the doctrine of predestination ... Fallen and rebellious humanity is utterly impotent to come unaided to the saving knowledge of God for which we were created. It is not a question of asking how we shall reconcile ourselves to God, but rather of receiving the reconciliation God has accomplished.'[10]

The reason Christians can accept such a view where God is everything and man nothing, is that they have already been persuaded that human nature has been fatally wounded in the 'Fall', that humans are 'dead in trespass and sins' (Ephesians 2:1) and that no one can seek God unless God first seeks them. It is this strange understanding of the human dilemma that naturally gave rise to the doctrine of predestination where God predetermines who will be saved and who not, a doctrine totally abhorrent to any rational-minded person. That same doctrine appeared in our analysis of the Reformed or Calvinistic Faith which I have already dealt with. It is the antithesis of the Jewish view which freely invites all people to seek after God and which believes that the way is always open for human beings to approach their Creator. The 'Old' Testament is filled with such invitations. 'Seek the Lord while he may be found, call upon him while he is near; let the wicked forsake their way, and the unrighteous their thoughts; let them return to the Lord, that he may have mercy on them, and to our God, for he will abundantly pardon' (Isaiah 55:6,7).

If we disallow Christians for putting their own spin on this verse, it stands as a clear, unqualified invitation that respects human independence and ability to make right choices. Whatever Judaism has understood by the story of the 'Fall' in Eden, it has never concluded from that story that human nature is hopelessly corrupted and incapable of turning towards God. It is significant that when Jesus told the story of the Prodigal Son, he told an essentially Jewish story. The apostle Paul would have had to tell it very differently.

McGrath is committed to the traditional doctrine that the essential Christian message or 'Gospel' is that 'God offers us salvation as a gift through the death and resurrection of Jesus Christ.'[11] Even though we have seen that in Judaism, the 'sinner' sincerely repents and God in response forgives, McGrath decries this idea as an inversion of the order of salvation. After all, if repentance is all God requires in order to forgive us, then God would not need to offer us the 'gift' of Christ's death. Forgiveness can't be dependent on repentance as the Jewish Scriptures say it is, because that would contradict the whole strange, often enigmatic scheme of salvation that Paul has created. 'To suggest that forgiveness is conditional, depending upon renewal and regeneration, is to abandon a crucial insight of the Gospel and to degenerate into some kind of moralism, such as that associated with the Enlightenment of the Eighteenth century.'[12] He really is not a fan of the Enlightenment, primarily because it took a healthier, more balanced and positive view of human nature and potential. He is not obviously concerned with Judaism in these statements, so he does not have to explain how his idea of forgiveness is at odds with that of the Old Testament prophets—and even of Jesus.

The only way historically, that Christianity could have emerged from Judaism as a distinct and unique religion was to offer a form of salvation that differed from the traditional, biblical form. The tragic death of Jesus was transformed into God's way of salvation. The Jews then and still today, wondered why God had changed his mind about the way he saves people. Knowing that absolutely everything depends on this teaching of vicarious atonement, McGrath states bluntly that 'If this belief is false, the Christian faith must be recognized as a delusion—a deeply satisfying delusion, to be sure, but a delusion none the less.'[13] I do not doubt that it *is* a delusion. What puzzles most atheists is why, for so many, it remains a 'deeply satisfying delusion'?

Who Speaks for God?

*'If we stop trying to establish the independent existence
of a supernatural reality that overwhelms us from outside,
we are left with the profound fact of the depth and richness of
our own unconscious from which insights and challenges emerge
into our minds. The revelations of our religious imagination are
among the most powerful of our creations ... all the ladders
start in our own heart'*

–Richard Holloway

The short answer is, almost everyone! The only 'person' who doesn't seem to speak for God—is God. As far as the real plights of humankind are concerned, God appears to be completely indifferent and uninvolved. Salvation may have everything to do with the world to come, but God doesn't seem too concerned with the world of the here and now. Richard Carrier in his essay *Why I am Not a Christian*, offered four reasons for not believing in the God hypothesis: God is silent, God is inert, the evidence is inadequate, and, Christianity predicts a different universe.[1]

The first two reasons alone are enough to prove that God is the product of our fertile human imagination rather than being a separate, self-existing entity. It is *we* who do all the talking for God, *we* who put words in his mouth, *we* who create the holy books or scriptures that purport to be his 'sacred word'. This is why, as humankind progresses and standards of universal morality improve, religion must always be busy qualifying words set down on stone or parchment millennia ago. *That* God cannot keep up, even with the behaviour, outlook and understanding of his feeble creatures and so his followers and spokespeople must be constantly re-interpreting what he said and meant in former times.

During my years as a minister of the Church, I often found myself confronted by difficult situations that needed some kind of comment. Whether it was the sudden, unexpected death of a member of the congregation, a natural disaster or some other account of terrible suffering, ministers are expected to comment and bring the word of God to bear on the subject. I remember two occasions in particular. One was the death of an African woman and mother who had come to Sydney with her husband for his academic studies. He planned to return to Ghana and use his studies and skills in the service of his country. Both attended our church and their third child was born during the time they lived in our community.

Shortly after returning to Ghana we received the terrible news that the mother had been killed in a bus accident, though the youngest child survived. I conducted a memorial service in Sydney with the congregation while the family grieved in Ghana. It was difficult to say anything encouraging or comforting at the service when I felt personally so bewildered and even disappointed—in God. Like most such incidents it made no sense, served no purpose and seemed such a waste of all the time and energy this devout Christian couple had put into their experience in Australia. This is hardly an uncommon experience for either believers or non-believers. The difference is, that as a believer and a minister or spokesperson for God, I was obliged to say *something* that involved God in the situation. God is supposed to have a plan or a purpose. He is supposed to be with us always, guiding, blessing and comforting, but we didn't feel much comfort.

The second occasion occurred in more recent times when Typhoon Haiyan, known in the Philippines as Typhoon Yolanda, slammed into that island country in November 2013. It was one of the strongest tropical cyclones ever recorded and when it struck it was devastating. It was the deadliest Philippine typhoon recorded in modern history, causing catastrophic damage and killing at least 6,300 people. We had already witnessed reports of the 2004 Indonesian Tsunami that killed more than 230,000 and injured more than half a million, but in 2013, one of the young women in our congregation received news that several members of her family had been swept away in the Philippines calamity.

On the Sunday immediately following, I presented a short powerpoint segment of scenes from the disaster accompanied by quotes from the book of Psalms, all protesting to God, asking him 'why'? and wondering what he was doing—or not doing. The Psalms are wonderful in that regard because they express every human emotion, and their author was not afraid to ask God difficult questions. Instead of trying to say something pious or comforting, I simply let the images and the quotes speak for themselves. A few days after presenting that segment during my morning service, I received a circular email letter from a Christian missionary friend in the Philippines. She spoke of the devastation, but also of how people had come to Christ as a result of the disaster. She also said that her Christian community strongly believed that God would be 'glorified' through all that had happened. This was an instance of saying too much. Reluctant as I was to sound contentious, I wrote to her and after explaining my own initial reactions to the tragedy, asked her to explain to me how she thought people would be converted or God would be glorified in all of this. Some weeks later she reassured me that she would respond to my questions at a later date. More than three years later, I have received no such response. What could she possibly say to support or defend such dubious and inappropriate claims?

Now of course most Christians know perfectly well why some of these things happen. They know about accidents and tectonic plates and the arbitrary ways of nature. They are not uneducated people. They know that we live in an imperfect world and that bad things happen to good people. They know in effect, what most non-believers know. But unlike the non-believer, they also 'know' that God rules over all, that he has a purpose for all our lives and that he is supposed to care for us, protect us. That's a harder knowledge to fit into the picture.

Some, though not all, also believe that all these natural disasters and horrors are the result of the 'Fall' of Adam in Eden. Through Adam's sin, death and suffering have entered the world. 'We live in a fallen world' Christians will say mournfully, without realising that this simply makes the matter worse because it implies that it is all *our* fault. Apparently in the perfect world God first created and placed us in, there were no accidents and no shifting tectonic plates. People didn't get sick and didn't die. I suppose I must have suggested something along those lines in the first years of my ministry, but gradually distanced myself from the idea that Typhoon Yolanda was our fault because we inherited Adam's 'original sin' and changed the natural world. What a sin that must have been!

I use these two examples of a mother's death in Ghana and a typhoon in the Philippines to explain why, increasingly, I used to get annoyed with God, even disappointed with God. A minister can feel that way but it is probably best not to share those feelings—though I did from time to time. It seems others felt the same way. What I was trying to say in all my conflicted emotions and thoughts was that I was sick of trying to explain God's ways or defend his actions (inactions?) and wished for once he'd speak for himself.

Why did it always have to be so damn mysterious? Why did we have to passively resign to his 'inscrutable will' and summon the faith to trust God regardless? Why would the answers only be forthcoming in the hereafter, but never in this world? Why did 'walking by faith' often seem like walking blind or irrationally, believing without any evidence to support that belief? Why were all the 'reasons' we gave for God's seeming inaction and lack of concern really reasons we ourselves concocted? Where were the chapters and verses of scripture that confirmed these reasons? Why, given hundreds of pages of Scripture, did God's holy word fail to provide us with any substantial explanation for the situations which confronted us.

Most of our funeral service sermons or 'messages of comfort' stuck to the tried and true verses from the Gospel of John or Paul's epistle to the Romans or First Corinthians. Had not Jesus on his last night with the disciples told them: 'In my Father's house there are many dwelling places. If it were not so, would I have told you that I go to prepare a place for you? … . I will come again and take you to myself, so that where I am, there you may be also' (John 14:1-4). That was always a comfort, but it didn't really answer any of our questions about the meaning of life or what happens when we die. After announcing this hope of a heavenly place, Thomas, bewildered, said to him: 'Lord, we do not know where you are going. How can we know the way'? That was a great opportunity for Jesus to provide some substance to his nebulous hope. Instead he uttered those mysterious words, 'I am the way, and the truth, and the life. No one comes to the Father except through me'. Nothing about the place Jesus was going to or how a dead—and hopefully resurrected body—would get there. Nothing but the assertion that the way of salvation is exclusively tied to the Savior Jesus. John's Gospel, written seventy or more years after the death of Jesus appears to put words into Jesus' mouth he probably never said. The famous 'I am' statements appear in none of the three earlier gospels. But even if he did say such things, we are still left pretty much in the dark as far as our real questions are concerned.

Jesus said 'I will come again and take you to myself'. He obviously didn't mean the disciples. They were all long gone before John composed these words in his gospel. Nor could he have meant the approximately eighty generations that were to follow. He didn't come back for any of them either.

And whoever wrote the last book of the New Testament, where the 'resurrected' Jesus says, 'Surely I am coming soon' (Revelation 22:20), has disappointed believers for centuries who took 'soon' seriously. But this is what faith is, it is 'the assurance of things hoped for, the conviction of things not seen' (Hebrews 11:1), and this is why it still provides comfort at Christian funerals. Because faith is regarded as such a noble, even heroic virtue, it is considered disrespectful to suggest that it is merely 'wishful thinking'. I still feel emotional when I hear the music and words of Disney's *When you wish upon a star*. We would all certainly like to believe these words. We wished they might be true, but in reality, they are generally not.

> When you wish upon a star
> Makes no difference who you are
> Anything your heart desires
> Will come to you.
>
> If your heart is in your dream
> No request is too extreme
> When you wish upon a star
> As dreamers do.
>
> Fate is kind
> She brings to those who love
> The sweet fulfillment of
> Their secret longing ...

Faith is a secret longing. It wants to believe that a god will grant us our heart's desire. In the story and film *Pinocchio*, the character Jiminy Cricket sings this song at the beginning and end of the movie. It is all about how dreams can come true—as they do sometimes— as Pinocchio is transformed from a wooden puppet into a real boy. The song is used in Disney promotional campaigns because it 'represents the feeling they want their guests to have when they visit the Disney theme parks'. Sadly, life is not a theme park, though some of the religions we create do obviously produce the same feelings Disney hoped his Disneyworld would generate.

Another much-used verse at Christian funerals is from St. Paul's epistle to the Romans. Speaking of the life and world to come and knowing that many of his people are suffering hardship and persecution, he tells them that, 'I consider that the sufferings of this present time are not worth comparing with the glory about to be revealed to us' (8:18). Apart from the sense of imminent return of Christ—'about to be revealed to us'—he wanted the Christians of his time to believe that the salvation expected soon would render insignificant all the sufferings of this earthly world. We have had a long time to put that assertion into perspective. I found myself at times, unable to repeat this text when I thought that it sounded trite or grossly exaggerated in the light of some of the real sufferings that people in the world were experiencing. Apply it to any one of a hundred situations where people have suffered loss, heartache, devastation and unimaginable cruelty, and the words of Paul sound like they are asking us to take an awful lot on trust.

It is inconceivable that the uncounted victims of torture, war, famine, disaster, family loss, death of children, victims of genocide and mothers desperately nurturing babies dying in their arms in the midst of famine, would ever, in any imaginable future heaven, consider that what they suffered was not worth comparing with what they got in heaven. It is another example of how God is silent about our lives in this world and only hints at what they will be like in the next. Not much comfort there.

One of the things that gave me a sense of identity and purpose as a teenage Mormon, was the conviction that *God was not silent*. Though Mormonism is undoubtedly having problems convincing people of its message these days, there is no doubt that some of its distinctive claims are still appealing to many people. Foremost among those claims is that God has shattered the silence of centuries and spoken again through his servant, the Prophet Joseph Smith (1805-1844). The message of the 'Restoration' is that the Gospel of Jesus Christ has been restored to the Earth in these 'latter days', that the heavens have opened and that revelation is forthcoming again.

The extraordinary, enigmatic career of Joseph Smith is testament to the power of this idea. The fact that people want it to be true, want to believe that God still speaks and acts today, only adds to the appeal.

When I joined the Mormon Church in 1961, David O. McKay (1873-1970) was the Prophet and President of The Church of Jesus Christ of Latter-day Saints, the eighth to succeed the founder, Joseph Smith. The current prophet, Thomas S. Monson is number sixteen. Joseph Smith was about the same age I was when I joined the Church—fourteen—when he had his first vision in 1820 of the Father and the Son. They appeared to him in the 'Sacred Grove' in upper New York State. The question every child asks in Sunday school or scripture classes after hearing endless Bible stories, seemed to my young mind to have been answered definitively by Mormonism. To the 'why doesn't God do these kind of things today?' the Mormons answer confidently that he does! In these 'latter days' he has raised up a new prophet through whom he has revealed his will and established his Church anew on the Earth. Of course Mormonism is not unique in making such a claim. Raised as a boy in the Church of Scotland (Presbyterian) it was easy for me to make the comparison between traditional 'apostate' Christianity and God's 'true' Church.

The lack of living prophets in Christian churches (though numbers of Pentecostal-Charismatic churches have since re-introduced them) is thought by Mormons to be a serious deficiency. The operations of the Gospel and the means of salvation are simply not possible in their eyes without a living prophet who speaks for God and holds all the 'keys' of the Priesthood. The presence of these living prophets, in contrast to the dead, Old Testament ones, is that they create a direct link between the Church and God. Someone here on earth is God's spokesperson. If we need to know something or be guided in a certain way, God will instruct his people through the Prophet. One Mormon hymn expresses this belief, 'We thank thee O God for a prophet, to guide us in these latter days;

we thank thee for sending the Gospel to lighten our minds with its rays'.[2] These men hold ultimate authority until the day they die. Their words, if pronounced given by the Lord, take precedence over anything that has been said, believed or practised before.

In this sense they are roughly the equivalent of Roman Catholic popes when they speak *ex cathedra*. I say 'roughly' because no pope has ever claimed to give out new teachings or current words from God. They are seen rather, as guardians of the deposit of faith 'once and for all delivered to the Saints'. They may be 'infallible' in the sense that they are protected by the Holy Spirit from teaching error, but they are seldom inspired enough to proclaim any new doctrines. The doctrines of the Assumption of the Blessed Virgin Mary into Heaven by Pope Pius XII on November 1, 1950 in his Encyclical *Munificentissimus Deus*, and of the Immaculate Conception by Pope Pius IX in his Apostolic Constitution *Ineffabilis Deus*, December 8, 1854,[3] might be considered new doctrines, but the Catholic Church explains them as clarifications of teachings long accepted and believed by the faithful. What separates Mormon prophets from Catholic popes is that Mormon prophets are free to introduce new doctrine or Scripture.

The *Book of Mormon*, subtitled, *Another Testament of Jesus Christ*, and 'authored' by Joseph Smith is the most obvious example of new scripture. It was one thing to claim that God was speaking in our times, quite another to produce the evidence. The Book of Mormon, a kind of New World or American Old and New Testament covering at least 1,000 years of ancient American history, burst upon the scene in 1830, amidst widespread astonishment and controversy. Joseph Smith produced other works of scripture, including the *Doctrine and Covenants* which contains 138 revelations given by God, mostly to Joseph Smith in the mid-nineteenth century. Very much like a modern Muhammad, with his holy Qur'an—also made possible through the visitation of an angel—Joseph Smith was the messenger of God, with a new or revitalised message.

Questions about why the revelations to prophets appeared to have ceased with the death of the Prophet Joseph Smith have led, in recent times, to the Church adding several newer revelations to the *Doctrine and Covenants*. One is a vision received by the then Prophet Joseph Fielding Smith in 1918. Two others are actually 'Official Declarations' made by Wilford Woodruff in 1890, shelving the controversial practice of polygamy, and another in the name of Spencer W. Kimball dated 1978, announcing that God was now lifting the ban on black-Americans holding the priesthood. None of these additions record God's actual words speaking directly to his prophet as in the days of Joseph Smith. They are indirectly relating what the men themselves said God had led them to say. The heavens may have re-opened in 1820 or 1830, but they haven't remained quite so open since about 1844. This means that the claim to have 'living prophets' today has to be somewhat qualified.

The people of Nineteenth century America were the first recipients in 2,000 years—if we discount the words of God to Muhammad in the Seventh century A.D.—to hear the words of God speaking for himself.

> Hearken, O ye people of my church, saith the voice of him who dwells on high, and whose eyes are upon all men; yea, verily I say: Hearken ye people from afar; and ye that are upon the islands of the sea, listen together. For verily the voice of the Lord is unto all men, and there is none to escape; and there is no eye that shall not see, neither ear that shall not hear, neither heart that shall not be penetrated ...

> And the voice of warning shall be unto all people, by the mouths of my disciples, whom I have chosen in these last days. Behold, this is mine authority, and the authority of my servants and my preface unto the book of my commandments, which I have given them to publish unto you, O inhabitants of the earth ...

> Wherefore, I the Lord, knowing the calamity which should come upon the inhabitants of the earth, called upon my servant Joseph Smith, Jun., and spake unto him from heaven, and gave him commandments ... and power to translate the Book of Mormon ... .power to lay the foundation

of this church, and to bring it forth out of obscurity and out of darkness, the only true and living church upon the face of the whole earth, with which I the Lord, am well pleased ...

(*Doctrine and Covenants*, Section 1, revelation given through Joseph Smith at Hiram, Ohio, November 1, 1831).[4]

God apparently felt obliged to communicate in Seventeenth century English prose rather than contemporary Nineteenth century American. Perhaps Joseph Smith wanted his revelations to sound more like Scripture in the same way that many fundamentalist Christians today, believe that the King James Version is the only 'real' Bible translation. God wanted to speak for himself again and so, Mormons claim, he did through Joseph Smith. But what seems to be a reassuring and comforting feature of the Mormon Church, turns out to be a source of change, inconsistency and reversal in policy, practice and belief.

The legacy of the prophets is an odd and questionable one because successive prophets have introduced new teachings and/or abolished former teachings and practices. These include the doctrine of God, the practice of polygamy, abolishing the prohibition on giving the priesthood to Blacks and amendments to the sacred Temple *Endowment* ritual. In each instance, many Mormons found the changes, total reversals in teaching or the abandonment of things considered sacred, hard to follow. Some refused to accept them, hence the existence of groups like Fundamentalist Latter-day Saints who still practice polygamy. What groups like the Fundamentalists do may be illegal, but they deserve credit for being *consistent* Mormons.

If you have surrendered your judgment of such issues to a supreme authority, such as a prophet, a pope or an ayatollah, what are you to do but submit, or live a life that is less than *kosher*. Catholicism provides a case in point. Despite official teaching, millions of Catholics practice birth control and do not accept what their church teaches about other moral issues. For a pope to change the doctrine and practice of the church on matters like birth control or the ordination of women, he would have to take the risk of contradicting the teachings of his predecessors and therefore calling into question the authority of the Church as a whole. Mormons committed to the belief that there is a God and that he does actually speak through his prophet in Utah, find themselves in a dilemma. They must either accept the official teaching whether it is consistent with previous teaching or not, or question their whole belief system and leave it, which is what an increasing number are doing.

Those who still tentatively believe, but are not willing to leave are often accused of speaking 'against the Lord's anointed' which is a phrase easily justifying ecclesiastical tyranny. The late Mormon apostle Bruce R. McConkie (1915-1985) responded to letters from confused Mormons asking why he had said that the curse on Blacks (regarded as descendants of Cain; denied the priesthood or any office in the church) could not be changed in this world; why he previously chastised Mormons who suggested that the ban or practice *ought* to be changed. He rebuked members reluctant to accept the new 1978 revelation abolishing the prohibition: 'People write me letters and say, 'you said such and such, and how is it now that we do such and such?' All I can say is that it is time disbelieving people repented and got in line and believed in a living, modern prophet. Forget everything I have said, or what President (Prophet) Brigham Young or whomsoever has said in days past that is contrary to the present revelation ... We spoke with a limited understanding ... It doesn't make a particle of difference what anybody ever said about the Negro matter before the first days of June of this year (1978).'[5]

This rather harsh statement has been endlessly quoted as an example of the inconsistent and dictatorial style of Mormon leadership. It remains a classic example of Mormon double-think. It also illustrates a fundamental difference between a religious and secular worldview. When humanity grows in its understanding of human rights and justice, it changes its laws and practices. Whether it is the treatment of women, the issue of slavery, social justice or homosexuality, societies make significant changes of attitude. They extend human rights. They abolish previous statutes and laws. They decriminalise certain human activities and actively promote the universal welfare of all members of their society. Religions by contrast are often unable to make similar changes because they are committed to belief in a God who has already said what he thinks of these things and cannot be seen to change his mind.

The abolition of slavery was not primarily a religious initiative. Indeed, religion has more often than not justified such a practice. The Christians of South Africa believed they could justify their white supremacy and apartheid on the basis of their Christian heritage and the Bible's teaching. Female suffragettes were as much opposed by Christian males as they were by their secular counterparts. God had ordained 'roles' for men and women, and society would suffer if those roles were changed. Homosexuality is clearly condemned in Scripture, women are to 'remain silent in church' and not 'exercise authority over men', so the Church cannot readily change its stance on homosexuality or women in the ministry.

The only way you can make changes in these areas is through what Christian critics of the liberals in their midst call *stretchegesis*. The Greek word *exegesis*, from the Greek for 'to lead out' or draw out, means 'a critical explanation or interpretation of a text, particularly a religious text'. Use of the invented term 'stretchegesis' means that those who question or re-interpret traditional views of Scripture on women or homosexuals, or the age of the earth, are guilty of stretching the text beyond any reasonable sense. God's word cannot be questioned, as Galileo and others discovered to their detriment.

When it *is* questioned and when churches do make amendments or re-interpretations of their doctrine, they are, in effect, correcting God. Theologians will always fall back on the old defence or excuse that it is our *understanding* of God's word which has changed, not the word itself. However it accommodates to reason, changing circumstances or scientific fact, religion must do so with the march of time or be relegated to total irrelevance and obsolescence. The best solution to this recurring dilemma would be for God himself to say something and propose a kind of religious first or second or third amendment to the Bible, but that is not going to happen. *People* do that sort of thing whether God approves or not. They hope he does approve, but since he remains silent, they can never be sure. When the Mormon prophets enlisted God's support for changes and asserted that God himself had authorized them, they provoked nothing but confusion and dissension, so there is no guarantee that 'new' revelation will help religion out of this dilemma.

A few years ago, my wife and I were touring in Salt Lake City, Utah and visiting all the key Mormon Church sites. When we toured the Beehive House next to Temple Square, I wondered how long it would take before the young female missionary guide would touch on the matter of polygamy. After all we tourists were sitting in *one* of Brigham Young's very large historic houses built especially to accommodate his twenty-eight wives and fifty-six children. Pictures of his wives were hanging on the walls. There was a tinge of nervousness when our guide who had been telling us the story of the Mormon Church, spoke briefly of the practice of plural marriage and then immediately informed us of the termination of that practice when it was judged 'no longer necessary'.

I remember those words, 'no longer necessary' and was itching to ask, why it was ever necessary in the first place? I declined to interrupt her presentation with any confronting or discomforting comments. It remains a valid question however, and could be asked of several of the other historic changes in Mormon history. Why were all these additional doctrines and practices, most unknown throughout Christian history, necessary? Mormonism is a relatively new world religion, just under two hundred years old, so it is easier to study its origins, development and present state, but many of these same questions could be asked of Christianity as well.

To those outside of Mormonism with some insight into the dynamics of this evolving faith and the way it deals with internal tensions and difficulties, it is not a mystery that it is constantly faced with unresolved problems. It is a mystery for many Mormons who deserve better than the feeble explanations provided by their hierarchy. Mormons note one troubling trend in all the changes. The teachings or doctrines that are changed or abandoned, are always the things that have caused the Church trouble or made it difficult to co-exist with the wider, non-Mormon culture. Instead of defending established doctrines or expanding on what has already been 'revealed', Mormon prophets periodically do away with things which have been difficult to maintain and promote.

Whether it has been polygamy, discrimination against African-Americans or disturbing elements of the secret Temple ritual, in each instance no revelation has ever been published stating the reasons for the changes. Curiously, God is not allowed to speak for himself. Instead, Mormons are to assume that revelation has been given by God to the presiding brethren or the prophet, but for reasons known only to them, the details of the changes are not for public consumption or scrutiny. You must simply trust the leaders who do as God directs.

This is an illustration of what I call the 'inventor's dilemma'. Humans invent religion and ascribe to God what they believe should be taught. With the passage of time and the changing circumstances of any given society, religious teachings need revising or updating. The Bible prohibition on the practice of usury or command to burn witches, stone disobedient children and adulterers, not violate the Sabbath day, sell all you have to give to the poor, not allow divorce and so on, have all had to be either abandoned or qualified. In each instance, the humans who created the teachings have to come up with reasons, sometimes ingenious or more often ingenuous, for that abandonment or qualification. Christianity is just as guilty of this as Mormonism. No Christian today could bear to live his or her faith in Elizabethan England or Calvin's Geneva. Most of the circumstances that have made life more civilized, tolerant and humane have come from secular and Enlightenment movements and not from God announcing changes to his 'eternal word.' So again, who speaks for God? We do.

James A. Lindsay has written a book called *God Doesn't; We Do: Only Humans Can Solve Human Challenges* (2012). In his discussion of the 'problem of a silent God' Lindsay says, 'We are forced to wonder why it is that a being that allegedly used to interact with human beings often, when we were superstitious and saw gods in every rock, weather event and change of circumstances, *now never does*, although the claim on his insistence in our credulity is as loud as ever.'[6] In the face of all contemporary claims for God being active in the world, or speaking through his appointed clergy or scriptural word, Lindsay rightly states that 'There is no evidence to counter the claim of God's silence.'

An institution like Mormonism which more and more looks like it was built on a shaky foundation, has constantly revised, changed, edited and censored its formative documents, history, revelation and theology. This is not something which you would expect of a religion freshly revealed from heaven less than two hundred years ago. It is a bewildering spectacle for anyone closely studying its history and character. Even today, there are records in the Church's archives which are not accessible to even Mormon scholars and researchers. Every religious movement has skeletons in its closet, periods and incidents it regrets or is deeply ashamed of. Mormonism just seems to have more of its fair share.

Mark P. Leone once wrote about the 'continuous revision of meaning' that lies at the heart of Mormonism. He spoke of it as a 'religious system full of unresolved difficulties' and described the Mormons as 'a rational population without a memory', meaning that 'the lack of a coherent, systematic interpretation of the relationship between the past and the present' leads Mormons to think that the way it is, is the way it always was.'[7] My own recent visit to Temple Square in Salt Lake City left me feeling that so much of the spectacular imagery and portrayal of Mormonism is frustrating and disturbing. A story is being endlessly told, re-crafted and promoted, but it is not the truth, the whole truth and nothing but the truth. What Leone said about Mormonism could just as readily be said about Christianity over its long, torturous, often puzzling history. If God is indeed speaking, he is a very poor communicator.

The silent God makes no attempt to clarify his original or any subsequent communications. One religion succeeds another or continues to co-exist with others, but there is no guidance from God as to which one we should all follow. All the religions have god or gods speaking with different voices, saying different things, but God himself will not tell us what he thinks. Christianity regards Mormonism as unorthodox, heretical and disconnected from historic Christian roots. It regards Mormon scriptures as false scriptures, not having the same inspiration or authority as the Bible. It does not consider Mormon prophets to be God's anointed servants.

But Mormonism does regard itself as Christian. In fact it proclaims itself as the 'restored' expression of the original Christian Church. This is why it calls itself 'The Church of Jesus Christ of *Latter-day Saints*'. It's the church that Jesus started and its members are the 'saints' of the latter days as opposed to those of the first century. It claims that early Christianity became corrupted and was lost in those early centuries of the Christian era. The Western Roman church that emerged was and is an 'apostate' church without true authority to act in God's name as a channel of salvation. Mormonism is 'no mere dissenting sect', but regards itself as 'a real religious creation, one intended to be to Christianity as Christianity was to Judaism: that is, a reform and a consummation.'[8]

In order for Christians to appreciate how Mormons feel about being regarded as a later and erroneous version of Christianity, they need to remember how Jews feel about Christianity. Judaism does not regard Christianity as a legitimate development of the original revelation given to Abraham and Moses. Nor does it regard the New Testament as an authentic scripture comparable to the 'Old' Testament. For Judaism there is only one covenant between man and God and Christianity is not the 'new covenant.' As Christians regard the Book of Mormon as a fraudulent addition to the Bible, so Jews regard the New Testament as a fraudulent addition to the Bible. As Christianity considers itself to be a 'reform and consummation' of Judaism, so Mormonism considers itself to be a 'reform and consummation' of Christianity.

Judaism believes that the one God communicated with Moses and all the people at Sinai, more than 3,000 years ago (a foundation event that biblical archaeologists have found almost impossible to substantiate). If God has changed his mind about the nature and function of the original covenant then he ought to have made it as clear as he did at Sinai when all Israel witnessed the presence of the Lord on the holy mountain and received his word through Moses. Instead, a handful of disciples proclaimed their faith in Jesus as the Messiah and announced that he had risen from the dead. If God had wanted all of the Jews to believe the Christian message, he could have demonstrated the resurrection of Jesus in a wider, more public and less ambiguous manner. He didn't.

As a result, most Jews then either did not know about the resurrection, and those who did hear of it, did not believe it. If you are a Christian you feel that God must have vindicated your religion because it did succeed and it did grow to become the world's largest faith. Judaism didn't. But if you are Jewish, the fact that lots of people believe something doesn't make it true, though they must wonder why God allowed Christianity to grow and become dominant in the way that it did. When *will* God's promises to Israel's prophets be fulfilled? When will the real Messiah actually come?

If success and size are evidences of God's favour, then what are Jews and Christians to make of Islam? Islam regards itself as God's *final* revelation to the world, with the holy Qur'an superseding and perfecting what was corrupted and lost in the Bible. And rather than seeing itself as a religion which began six hundred years after Christ or almost seventeen centuries after Judaism, Islam announces that it is a restoration or continuation of the *original* covenant God made with Abraham. Muslims are the 'children of Abraham'. Abraham was the first Muslim! Just as Mormonism gave itself a sacred heritage of antiquity in the 'historical' record of the Book of Mormon, so Islam gave itself a sacred antiquity in making a direct connection with Abraham.

It also, like Christianity, absorbed the 'Old' Testament scripture as part of its own worldview. Just as Jesus was God's final word—'Long ago God spoke to our ancestors in many and various ways by the prophets, but in these last days he has spoken to us by a Son whom he has appointed heir of all things' (Hebrews 1:1-2)—so Islam reveres Muhammad as the 'seal' of the prophets, God's final and ultimate messenger. The three great monotheistic faiths are thus locked into an inextricable and uneasy bond.

Why, the curious observer might ask, did God allow Muhammad to come up with a different version of religion that would grow as rapidly as it did, consume all the historic Christian centres in the East and, while starting centuries later, catch up to such an extent that today it is the second-largest religion in the world? Why, when the Prophet retired to that cave outside Mecca, didn't God send the Angel Gabriel to tell him that Jesus was God's final word to the world and that he should unite the Arab peoples with their Christian neighbours? For that matter, since Muhammad was well acquainted with sizeable Jewish communities in Arabia, why didn't God tell him that he should unite himself with that community and become part of the covenant God had made through Abraham and Moses? Why?

The Jewish prophets are speaking. Christian apostles and evangelists are speaking. Muhammad is speaking. They are all saying different things and their different interpretations of the truth and of salvation will lead to centuries of conflict, persecution and suffering. But God remains silent. If you are a believer, say a Christian, then you must accept that it is all part of God's great plan. He planned for Christianity to supplant Judaism as a 'light to the nations'. He planned somehow for Islam to be part of the development of civilization. Or perhaps he didn't. Perhaps he *was* speaking but Muhammad misunderstood. Or worse still, perhaps the Devil is the author of the other religions and he deceived Muhammad by appearing as an angel of light.

Liberal Christians tend to see all religions as paths to God, with some being more enlightened than others, but all possessing a measure of the truth. In this scenario, it does not ultimately matter which religion you belong to, as long as you sincerely seek God. That isn't quite the message of the New Testament, but it is an appealing idea. More conservative Christians, less tolerant of error, tend to think that for something like Islam to have become as big and successful as it has, it must have had supernatural assistance. But in this instance, the supernatural is demonic. There is scriptural precedent for this kind of thinking. Paul in his second epistle to the Corinthians warns against 'false apostles' who lead the people astray. These charlatans 'want an opportunity to be recognized as our equals'. The fact that such 'deceitful workers' appear so spiritual and lead people astray, should not surprise us says Paul. 'Even Satan disguises himself as an angel of light. So it is not strange if his ministers also disguise themselves as ministers of righteousness. Their end will match their deeds' (2 Corinthians 11: 12-15). Paul was talking about false apostles within the Christian community, most likely Jewish Christians who rejected his particular theology of the Cross. Islam didn't exist when he was preaching and writing, but his words have often been applied by Christians to other religious movements.

It is commonplace for example, for Christians to respond to the genius, mystery and extraordinary influence and success of the prophet Joseph Smith by saying that he was deceived by the Devil disguised as an angel of light. Both Islam and Mormonism began with the visit of an angel to their respective founding prophets. Gabriel visited Muhammad and Moroni visited Joseph Smith. Shouldn't that concern us, Christians ask? Didn't the apostle Paul warn us about that? 'There are some who are confusing you and want to pervert the gospel of Christ. But even if we or an angel from heaven should proclaim to you a gospel contrary to what we proclaimed to you, let that one be accursed!' (Galatians 1:7,8).

Unbelievers who see religion as a human construct, have less difficulty trying to account for the differing religions emerging through history. They never ask why God would allow such conflicting movements to come into being. They just did. God had nothing to do with it. The silent God is silent for the obvious reason that he doesn't exist. If he did, we might expect him to be a little bit more helpful and forthright in the face of all those different religions that are 'confusing you'. Remember, our eternal destiny depends on getting religion right. If we don't find the correct way to salvation, and it does turn out to be Christianity after all, then we could spend hundreds of millions of years—billions of years— in Hell. Whether Hell is literal fire and brimstone or C.S. Lewis's seemingly more bearable but no less terrifying grey town of endless monotony and regret where 'the debris of a decayed human soul finds itself crumpled into ghosthood'[9], God must surely want us to avoid such a fate.

Of course he does, pleads the Christian. 'God our saviour wants everyone to be saved and to come to the knowledge of the truth' (1 Timothy 2: 4). Such a sentiment stands in stark contrast to Reformed or Calvinist theology which emphasizes God's 'Eternal decrees' in which he sovereignly chooses the number of the saved and the number of the damned. Many other Christian traditions however do sincerely believe that God does want everyone to be saved. Which still begs the question, if that is the case, then he could have done far more to encourage 'everyone' to believe. Not staying silent for starters would be a big help.

When I was troubled about the relationship between the Old and New Testaments years ago, I visited with my professor of Old Testament at Morling College in Sydney. My concern was with how Paul said one thing about the Jewish Law, but the 'Old' Testament said quite another. How, according to the older scripture was the law a 'tree of life' and 'sweeter than honey to the soul', while according to the New Testament it was an 'instrument of death' which condemned those who observed it to God's judgment? It was all about Paul trying to show how Christianity was replacing Judaism. My professor offered some explanation which I did not find convincing, but concluded that for him, the *real* question that most troubled him, was the Church's response to the 'others'. He believed that in the Twenty-first century the greatest issue facing Christianity would be the creation of a credible explanation for how other world religions fit into God's scheme of things, how they get 'saved'. The real question was about salvation. That I could agree with.

John Hick is one theologian who addressed this question more often than most. In 1995 he published *The Rainbow of Faiths: Critical Dialogues on religious Pluralism*. He did what my professor said we needed to do, he took a hard look at this important intellectual problem facing all Christians today. As the blurb on the back cover of the First American Edition asks: 'Where exactly does Christianity fit into the scheme of the world in light of other world religions? And is it possible to remain Christian while accepting the truth of other beliefs? Offering good reasons for why the traditional stance that Christianity is the only true religion is no longer workable, Hick puts forth a cogent defense of Christianity in the global context of other religions.'[10] Both Hans Kung and John Hick have been prominent in helping people to think intelligently about this question.

Hick reminds Christians of the unsettling truth that 'there is no evidence that Christians live in a closer relationship with God than those outside Christianity'.[11] Most Christians I have known are well aware of this fact and it does lead some to ask how God's so-called 'grace' really works in the life of Christians. How is their being 'born again' or regenerated by the Holy Spirit's power, or 'being in Christ' make any difference? Lots of reasons (excuses) are given, but as Hick suggests, 'theology's function is to make sense of the facts, not to be a device for systematically ignoring or contradicting them'.[12]

Hick also agrees with the conclusion I drew earlier that some Christian expressions of salvation make God a monstrous, amoral deity. 'Only fundamentalists believe that God condemns the majority of the human race who have never encountered the gospel, to eternal damnation. Such a god would be the devil'.[13] As a liberal, Hick draws on analogies like the 'duck-rabbit' or two-dimensional maps to make the point that reality is differently perceived and that all theologies, of whatever religion, 'must always be inadequate representations of the reality', that 'the *real* is capable of being humanly thought of and experienced in more than one way'.[14] He speaks of an 'ultimate divine reality, which is being differently conceived and therefore differently experienced'.[15]

As I have said before, I always found such an approach to be more reassuring than the narrow dogmatism I was first exposed to. But in the end, the result is always a move in the direction of agnosticism. The God of the liberals is always 'transcendent', 'ineffable', 'ultimate reality'. Hick cleverly says that 'The Real is no *thing*, but not nothing!' Ordinary people struggling to understand what that means, can't be blamed for finding this version of religion elusive and hard to experience. Hick explains his view:

> It is not a *thing* because it transcends all our thing-concepts, including our religious thing-concepts. But on the other hand it is not nothing: it is that reality in virtue of which, through our response to one or other

of its manifestations as the God figures or the non-personal Absolutes (of Eastern religions), we can arrive at the blessed unself-centred state which is our highest good'.[16]

Billy Graham would have had no responses to his invitations for people to come forward and commit themselves at his huge crusades, if he had invited them to accept 'the blessed unself-centred state which is (your) highest good'. Instead, he invited them to come forward and receive Christ, the Saviour who once lived on earth, died for their sins and rose from the dead to intercede for them on high. Christianity believes its great strength and unique nature is that it proclaims a God who has revealed himself in Jesus Christ, who actually saves them by his personal actions on their behalf. This makes it easier for Christians to say that God does speak, does show himself and has made himself clear. People still have to choose to believe that the transcendent God could actually become a human being and also limit his public life to a very tiny geographical area and one particular people in the first century A.D. for a very brief period of time of one to three years. If Jesus really was God speaking to us, then it seems a highly inefficient and unconvincing way to show that he 'wants everyone to be saved'.

Whatever people think of Jesus, they still have to wonder about God the Father. Why does *he* appear to remain silent and inert? Christians like to argue for the existence of God by offering Jesus as the proof, but that really is to put the cart before the horse. You have to establish first that a god exists and then consider the evidence for that god having become a human being. Since Jesus never clearly identified himself *as* God, but was always careful to draw a distinction between himself and God, the question of God's existence remains.

Hick is aware that the 'truth' that Jesus of Nazareth was God incarnate and that his atoning death provided salvation, 'has never been available in practice to more than a minority of human beings', and that 'the greater the benefit of being born into this divinely favoured segment of human history, the greater the injustice to those born outside it'. He calls this 'the scandal of restricted access which unhappily undermines every religious value that we can attribute to the incarnation doctrine'.[17] It is an indisputable fact that in today's world, religious belief is largely determined, as it always has been, by geography. Millions are born in particular regions of the world with particular cultures and it is the family, tribe, clan, society and dominant religion which creates religious identity. God must have known that this would be the case, but instead of instigating some arrangement that would have resulted in a more universal enlightenment, he has chosen to 'allow' the present development of human society to continue.

Did God know that China would end up with the largest population of humans, that more of us are Chinese than anything else? Then why didn't he call a Chinese Abraham out of ancient Anyang (1600-1046 B.C.) and have a Chinese Jesus born during the Han Dynasty (206 B.C.—220 A.D.). If a later Chinese emperor had adopted the religion of this Chinese Christ as Constantine, the Roman Emperor adopted the religion of the Christian Christ, then Christianity would probably constitute at least two-thirds of today's human population. If God really does want 'everyone' to be saved, wouldn't China have been a better bet than Judaea? What about India with the second largest human population in the world? Rather than 'allow' Hinduism to evolve during the almost impenetrable past of the sub continent, God could have made the Indians his 'chosen people' and Christ instead of Krishna would be the most adored deity there today. But God remained silent through all of Indian history as well.

Worse than that, five hundred years before Jesus was born, that other Christ-like figure, Gautama Buddha, brought his message of enlightenment to all of India. After all Siddhartha's searching for the truth, why didn't God intervene and tell him that the 'truth' was already revealed through the prophets of Israel and Judaea or that centuries after Siddhartha's death the promised one who would bring salvation once and for all, would be born in the Middle East? Why did he 'allow' Buddha to achieve enlightenment, an enlightenment that was neither received nor 'revealed' but came from the Buddha's own heart and mind? Why 'allow' this great soul to admonish people to find their own way, to achieve their own 'salvation' and not to be concerned with the question of whether gods exist or not? But as the Buddha sat under the Bodhi tree in Bodh Gaya, India, God apparently remained silent again. The result, half a billion Buddhists today who do not need God or a saviour-Christ, but seek and find their own way to enlightenment.

The unbeliever observing the march of human history and progress concludes that all these religious movements were creations of the human mind and imagination. Their rich diversity represents the diversity of humanity itself. No need to ask why God was silent or less directive than he should have been. God had nothing to do with any of it. 'Aren't theologians really just playing the role of God's translators, and every holy book ever written in merely a detailed psychoanalysis of God?'[18]

By declaring itself as the only true religion Christianity creates a dilemma about the fate of the 'others' that has never been resolved. It hasn't been resolved by liberals or universalists because then the atoning death of Christ makes little sense. It hasn't been resolved by the conservatives because most Christians instinctively find the problem an unsettling one. Few I assume, at least in my own experience, cavalierly dismiss the billions outside of Christ without any sense of the injustice of it all, or without any inclination to question the character of God. Hick has put the problem in very stark and very honest terms.

> We see the negative fact that most of the world is non-Christian, but also (we see) the positive fact that most who are not Christian are of faiths other than Christianity. This makes the scandal of restricted access doubly scandalous; for insistence upon the unique revelation of God's love and co-suffering with humanity in Jesus downgrades the other great world faiths to the status of derivative or lesser revelations

and/or unconscious and secondary conduits of Christian salvation. I have argued in line with much contemporary thinking, that this traditional superiority claim is religiously unrealistic; and indeed I think that scepticism and discomfort about it is very widespread today among thoughtful Christians.'[19]

The problem of religious pluralism, a problem that confronts every Christian in almost every Western society in which immigrants have made their home, is a problem that will only intensify with the passage of time. It is part of Christianity's Achilles heel. Hick compares the impact of this question of the fate of the 'others', with the impact felt in the second half of the nineteenth century when the fact of biological evolution challenged the Christian worldview, 'setting up a painful conflict with the inherited orthodoxy'. The reaction against this challenge was 'powerful and prolonged', and we might add, that for millions of fundamentalist Evangelicals the reaction continues unabated. But in the end, as we all know, truth prevailed and the churches had to re-interpret their theology and their understanding of Genesis in the light of the new science. Hick observes that 'the human mind adjusts itself to reality, even if often only slowly and reluctantly', and he believes that the same painful process will be repeated in the case of religious pluralism. Christians will have to accept that Christianity is 'one among a plurality of authentic human responses to the divine reality.'[20]

Such a conclusion, though more insightful and realistic does not auger well for the future of Christian faith. It is interesting how the two issues—biological evolution and religious pluralism—are linked. The first undermined the Christian belief in human origins and human nature. It effectively obliterated any credible idea of a 'Fall.' That meant that the role of Christ as saviour, reversing the effects of Adam's original sin, was rendered meaningless. The second crisis also threatens the unique role of Christ as saviour because it is all too evident that the majority, even the religious majority of the human race, seeks and claims to find God *apart* from Christ. If God is the grand engineer of human salvation behind Adam and Christ, then he has not, by any measure, been a successful God.

I have singled out Hick as the kind of theologian who is willing to attempt serious answers to very serious questions. The fact that many of his conclusions are closer to those of non-believers is beside the point. Hick more accurately than those who seek simple, straightforward, unexamined beliefs, represents the evolving nature of Christianity, perhaps of religious faith in general, and can be appreciated as an authentic voice of faith struggling to find some substance he can still believe in. Hick continued to the end of his life to promote his reconceptualization of the Christian Faith as he understood it. The ideas of the Trinity and of the two natures of Christ (one human and one divine), as well as the concept of substitutionary atonement were for him and, he believed, for most people, 'incomprehensible'.

Monster or Handbag?

We don't look to God anymore because few of us believe the old story anymore: that God pulls all the levers in the world, and will do so in our favour if we pray, pay and obey. The old Sunday school faith of 'all things bright and beautiful' is gone, since we now know from Charles Darwin how life evolved on earth through the long and violent struggle of 'nature red in tooth and claw', as Tennyson put it
—Scott Cowdell

In the final chapter of his book *God and the New Atheism*, theologian John F. Haught tells us that 'The point of Christian theology, Pope John Paul II wrote in his encyclical *Fides et Ratio,* is to explore the mystery of God's self-emptying love.'[1] That mystery is most sublimely expressed in the death and resurrection of Jesus Christ. In all we have surveyed in these pages about the meaning of Christ's death, it is both sobering and worrying to think that *this* is 'the point of Christian theology'.

No one, believer or non-believer, insists that we are capable of understanding everything. An element of mystery will always persist in this amazing universe and in the way we humans perceive it. But real mystery is different to the mysteries that the human mind concocts. We are living at a time in history when the depths of real mystery are being plumbed with ever-greater success. At the same time there is a growing impatience and criticism of the concocted mysteries that have always been the stock-and-trade of religion. We seem to be in the midst of a paradigm shift in our perception of the 'truth' that really makes us free.

For Christians, the symbol of the cross communicated a distinctive message to the ancient and eventually the Mediaeval world. It was the Christian way of saying *this* is the symbol of salvation, but not salvation as you have known it—in Judaism. Here is a fresh new message to be heard. The irony is that while this is certainly true today, and has been since the time of Constantine, for nearly four hundred years Christians purposely avoided representing Jesus nailed to a cross. Unlike most of the artistic depictions today, including jewellery, the actual image of Christ on a cross was of a man beaten, bleeding, stripped naked and writhing in agony on wooden cross beams. You did not want to remind the public that your Saviour was executed as a common criminal by the Roman authorities. Other, more subtle symbols like the fish, were far more commonly employed by the early Christians. *Ichthus* employed the first letters of the word for 'fish' in Greek, to represent, 'Jesus Christ, God's Son, Saviour'.

Then the emperor Constantine claimed that just prior to the Battle at the Milvian Bridge in 312, he saw the sign of the cross in the sky and was given the command to conquer by that sign—*in hoc signo vinces*. Once the emperor made Christianity a tolerated religion, stopped the persecution of Christians and lent imperial support and favour for the flourishing of the Christian religion, the sign of the cross became a badge of honour and triumph—as it had always been in the New Testament. It must forever remain a strange anomaly that the God of Heaven and Earth should ever have said to the supreme commander of imperial military forces, the legions of Rome, 'by this sign, *conquer!*' Now centuries later and despite immense familiarity with artistic and motion picture depictions of the cross of Christ, Christians, like their brethren centuries ago, are increasingly struggling with just how they ought to interpret this symbol and several of the doctrines associated with it.

Three theologians in Australia who have written on this struggle to understand the Christian faith and to explain the obvious decline in religious belief are Tom Frame, Mark D. Thompson and Scott Cowdell. Tom Frame was a former Bishop to the Australian Defence Force (2001-2007), former Director of St. Mark's National Theological Centre in Canberra, and is currently Director of the Australian Centre for the Study of Armed Conflict and Society (ACSACS). He is a prolific author with a particular interest in the Anglican Church. I have enjoyed all of his books and particularly *Losing my Religion: Unbelief in Australia* (2009). I know Tom personally, and remember him telling me that the title was not his idea because it gave the wrong impression that this bishop was losing his faith. The publisher's chose the title and it refers to the fact that Australians generally, are losing their faith. Unbelief is on the rise in Australia.

While still in the ministry when this book appeared, I found it insightful and helpful for understanding my own challenges in communicating the gospel to an increasingly indifferent and sceptical society. Reading it now, I also value it for the insights it gives non-believers who can benefit from knowing what Christians themselves are saying about why belief is in decline. While I have mainly been concerned with one particular Christian doctrine in this work, it may be helpful to end with how the great religious edifice is showing serious cracks.

Frame traces the decline in religious beliefs to a beginning in the 1950's. He cites several reasons which he says are unrelated to the existence and growth in Australia, of other faiths. 'Australians did not abandon the religion of their parents for the beliefs of the new arrivals.'[2] The reasons he gives are: the growth of alternative community organisations and clubs, most without religious affiliations; the collapse of the Sunday School movement and the demise of many large youth groups; the decline of tokenism and the end of nominalism; the demise of Sunday as the day of Sabbath rest as a range of cultural and sporting activities compete with church-going; an increase in the community's familiarity with alternative views of the natural world and embracing of naturalist, non-religious views of the Earth and human existence; the more open empathetic discussion of atheism and agnosticism coupled with disdain for religious extremism; the Church being out of touch with the latest scientific thinking and emerging cultural mores and its condemnation for reactionary and illiberal tendencies in opposing scientific research and restricting personal freedom; and lastly the Church's inability to speak with one clear voice on compelling issues. Significantly Frame stated that all these factors 'led many in the community to conclude that all religions were humanly contrived and that none spoke with divine authority'.[3] That of course, is precisely what numerous ex-ministers and Christians have come to believe.

Frame is somewhat dismissive of the popular publications of the new atheists. 'In my view their principal achievement has been to confirm the position of those who were already without religious belief or who found themselves among the ranks of disbelievers'.[4] There is some truth in that, but the same could also be said about the international, multi-billion dollar Christian publishing market. It is addressed largely to the converted and sustains itself only by producing endless variations on familiar themes and by creating Christian versions of secular concerns and issues.

The amount of Christian fiction, including fantasy, is growing apace, in an obvious response to that already existing market in secular society. Content is increasing exponentially whilst substance is often conspicuous for its absence. In my experience as someone who always encouraged my congregants to read and promoted the establishment of a library within the church building, only a minority of Christians showed any interest in reading. Frame has observed that, at least in Australia, 'Catechesis of individual believers is poor; apologetics is not a high priority', and 'The Christianity that most Australians have encountered is weak and insipid and, in more than a few instances, uninspiring and unintelligible.'[5] He adds, 'The residue of belief found among Australians is theologically deficient and philosophically unsophisticated'.[6]

This state of affairs, far worse in Western Europe I imagine, is largely blamed on changes in society and the failure of the church to engage, inform and inspire its adherents. As an analyst of Australian religious society, Frame has few equals, but unlike his more liberal counterparts, he is not willing to concede that some dogmas of the Church are in need of revision or abandonment. He laments, for example, the perception that 'the great religious questions of previous centuries can be safely ignored because the answers have been deemed irrelevant and marginalised'[7], and worries that 'In conflating secularism with atheism, the Australian state will eventually become anti-religious and lose the affections of those citizens who retain religious beliefs.'[8] As someone who has always been an advocate for the separation of church and state in a secular society and even supported the view that the Church of England should be dis-established in England, Frame seems overly pessimistic about the benefits of living in a more robust secular society where all religious beliefs are tolerated and the free practice of religion upheld in law.

Unlike other sociologists of religion, Frame is no mere academic observer and processor of facts and trends. One of the great strengths of this particular book is that it is infused with his personal reflections and confessions. Though disappointed that 'fewer persist in struggling with the questions until they arrive at satisfactory answers ... belief in God has been hard to sustain at times.'[9] He relates how, in order to strengthen his own faith and do justice to troubling questions, he studied world religions 'in order to ensure I hadn't been blinded to their insights' and that he took seriously, arguments against the existence of God. Apart from Scotland's ex-primus, Bishop Richard Holloway, I have never read a Bishop as honest and vulnerable as Tom Frame.

> There have been times when professing Christian belief has nearly driven me to despair. In darker moments I confess that religious faith torments my mind, mocks my judgments and burdens my spirit ... I feel at times, that wrestling with God is my vocation ... It is difficult to reduce belief to words and faith to concrete concepts. It is easier to explain why I have problems with believing and why faith is a wrestling with God.[10]

As the result of my own past wrestling with God, I differ from Frame in concluding that God's making it so difficult for us to believe in him, is not for the purpose of refining or perfecting our faith, but is evidence of his very real absence and non-existence. Frame outlines all the obvious issues that are 'the source of external despair'. He talks about 'the presence of so much suffering inflicted by humans upon humans, and not being able to arrive at reasonable expectations of what God could and should do'. He has seen at first hand, violence in East Timor, the Solomons, Palestine and Northern Ireland and confesses he does not know 'when or whether God should or would be expected to intervene'.

When he hears Christians mouth platitudes such as God being present in the sufferings of his people, he is honest enough to say that he does not know what this statement means, and that when Christians 'utter that other greater rejoinder: 'God is in control'', that 'it does not always appear to be so from my vantage point.'[11] Christians committed to a belief in the absolute 'sovereignty' of God seem to derive an immense amount of comfort and reassurance from that one platitude, 'God is in control.' When nothing makes sense, it is important for them to insist that there *must* be sense and since God exists, he must be in control. God cannot, it seems, be silent or inert enough, to convince believers to doubt that he is there, that he loves them and that he is in control.

Knowing Tom Frame as I did, while serving as a minister of a church, I feel that even now, as a non-believer, he and I are not so far removed. I suppose the difference between people like us, is that he continues to struggle with his belief in God, but I, convinced that a hidden, silent God is unworthy of my efforts to relate to him, have abandoned the struggle. Christians ask the same probing questions that atheists ask, they just refuse to accept that the implications of those questions are fatal to belief. Frame asks, 'While I don't believe God has abandoned the world, how is God's apparent absence to be understood?'[12] He has no final answers to all these issues that try his faith. 'My (only) recourse is reflection on the life of Christ.' And that is how his book ends.

Despite all the difficulties and problems associated with believing in God, he still feels confronted by Jesus Christ and believes that 'his dying and rising has transformed human history'. *How*, I could ask, has Christ transformed human history? An unredeemed world as Judaism continues to say, is clear evidence of the absence of a redeemer. It is testimony to the emotional and psychological impact of the *idea* of Jesus as the Christ, that someone like Frame can say that, 'When I am persuaded that the claims made about him are false, exaggerated or misunderstood, there will only be one alternative. I, too, will lose my religion.'[13] For myself, the greatest claim about Christ, that he was the saviour of a lost world, is unsustainable and unbelievable.

The second Australian theologian I want to consider, is also a member of the same Church Tom Frame belongs to, the Anglican Church of Australia. He is Mark D. Thompson, Principal of Moore College in Sydney, arguably the most influential theological college in the country. Though unrepresentative of the broader, more liberal Anglican community in Australia, the Sydney Diocese is the strongest and richest in terms of resources. It produces more candidates for parish ministry than any other college or seminary. It is also decidedly conservative and Reformed.

Thompson does not struggle with issues in the same way that Frame and others do. For him the message of the Gospel is more straight-forward and unambiguous. Despite being aware of the same decline in religious faith that Frame referred to, Thompson believes that Christians can be confident they have the truth and that it is the only truth worth proclaiming. 'The gospel is something that can be proclaimed. It is a message that confronts, challenges, informs and gives hope. It transforms life and turns the world upside down.'[14] Principal Thompson stresses that 'this message is not our message' (Galatians 1:11). It is not a human theological construct, the product of our thoughtful reflection upon what God has done in Jesus. It is God's message addressed to us'. Most importantly Thompson says, the message has its source in God's love for 'the world of human beings lost in sin. John 3:16.'[15] In the Sydney Anglican Diocese they do not 'tamper' with the message, nor do they feel themselves at liberty to 'redefine' it for a different age. They have no authority to 'omit part of it for any reason' and certainly not because someone might feel uncomfortable with it. This is the uncompromising message of Sydney Anglicanism which I touched on briefly in a previous chapter.

It is not perturbed by how intolerant, harsh or strange the gospel might sound to people, but confidently and fearlessly proclaims what the Bible says: 'There is salvation in no one else, for there is no other name under heaven by which we must be saved, Acts 4:12.' Starting again with the 'solution'—Christ's saving death, Thompson reminds us that the 'plight' of humankind is dire.

> The very idea of salvation implies a danger from which we are saved. What is that danger? Paul makes it crystal clear... 'The times of ignorance God overlooked, but now he commands all people everywhere to repent, because he has fixed a day on which he will judge the world in righteousness by a man whom he has appointed; and of this he has given assurance to all by raising him from the dead' (Acts 17:30-31).[16]

Like the Robinson family robot in the T.V. series *Lost in Space* who constantly exclaims, 'Danger, Will Robinson, danger!' when the boy is unaware of an impending threat, this conservative expression of Christianity feels obliged to remind us all of the danger facing our eternal souls. Thompson believes that the salvation Christ brings is 'salvation from the judgment and wrath of God before all else'. Just in case you may feel that the world is facing more serious and relevant problems and that we are too preoccupied with threats to *this* life to bother about possible threats in another life, Thompson tells us that, 'All other things, social disintegration, ecological catastrophe, political tyranny, economic loss, dashed hopes in so many areas—all other things pale in the light of salvation from the judgment and the holy, justified anger of the living God'.[17] He may not be a literalist when it comes to the age of the earth or the precise nature of the Fall in Eden, but he clearly subscribes unquestioningly to the idea of the fallen, corrupted nature of humankind—however it happened, so fallen and so corrupted that without divine intervention, we are all doomed to experience the 'justified anger of the living God'.

It is disturbing to hear how human beings who claim that this is not *their* message, but God's, can so blithely adopt such a pessimistic view of human nature in the name of that God, subscribing without question to all the false assumptions that the view entails. 'We are sinners who are active and responsible for the sins we have committed' he adds, and then unhesitatingly defends the honor of his offended God. 'The absolutely right and just and pure wrath of God at sin is exactly what we all deserve.'[18] Having previously seen how the doctrines of the Fall and of original sin in Kung's words 'can no longer be maintained', it is difficult to understand where such intensity and pessimism can still be coming from. It must be, as Sanders pointed out earlier, that having started with the 'solution', i.e. the premise that Christ is the Savior, Thompson is compelled to paint the 'plight' that his terrible death was meant to redress, in the bleakest of terms. You start with the worst possible news imaginable, so that the 'solution' sounds like immense relief or 'good news.' So while we deserve God's 'pure wrath', yet 'because of Jesus and his death and resurrection, those who are his are saved from 'the wrath to come'. That is the good news of the gospel.'[19]

Thompson makes the traditional Christian claim that such a gospel message did not just appear out of the blue with Jesus' preaching ministry, but had 'always been in God's mind, right from the beginning and the promise in the midst of the curse in the Garden' (Genesis 3:15). Judaism has long protested that such a plan of salvation pointing to Christ did *not* always reside in the mind of God. But like Islam claiming Abraham as a Muslim, this Christian theologian claims a phrase in Genesis as a foretelling of the sacrificial death of Christ. God speaking to the *serpent* following Adam and Eve's eating of the forbidden fruit says, 'I will put enmity between you and the woman, and between your offspring and hers; he will strike your head, and you will strike his heel'.

This is one of those fantastic Christian 'stretchegesis' of an ancient Hebrew text, where Christians presume to find Christ everywhere in the 'Old Testament', working backwards from the cross, to find reason and prediction of its occurrence. Some human offspring of the woman, Eve, will strike the serpent's head. But the serpent will strike that offspring's heel. *Obviously,* this is a prophecy predicting that Jesus will seriously wound the Devil by atoning for our sins on the cross, but the Devil will succeed in wounding Christ's heel, i.e. inspiring the crucifixion itself. Just think how many very dubious assumptions are made by reference to this text alone.

In order for Thompson to establish the case for our salvation from God's judgment and wrath, he subscribes to the existence of an actual Adam and Eve in a fabled Eden. He believes that a snake in the garden, one of God's creations, was the means of tempting Eve. He further believes that as a result of Eve and then Adam's disobedience, a 'curse' was placed on nature itself, the animal kingdom and Adam and Eve themselves. The only reason we know about this curse is because the book of Genesis records God talking to the snake and telling it that it was responsible for this calamity and would be 'cursed among all animals.' However loosely or imaginatively this is to be interpreted, even by Thompson, the basic elements of Genesis

3 are essential to providing the reason for God's terrible judgment and wrath. Thompson specifically cited the curse in the garden in Genesis 3:15 in order to explain the gospel. He can't for example, refer to the 'last Adam' (Christ) without implying the existence of a *first* Adam.

Since most Bible scholars and New Testament commentaries now agree that the central message of Jesus was about the coming of God's kingdom and the need for people to be ready and worthy to enter it, Thompson, momentarily gives space to that idea. 'We could reflect on how the gospel relates to the idea of God's kingdom, especially in Matthew's Gospel, where to speak of 'the gospel of the kingdom' was possibly more necessary because of the particular audience he had in mind'. This is a weak point, conceding what the real message of Christ was—a message consistent with all of the 'Old' Testament prophets—but insisting nevertheless, that 'while each of these things (other biblical themes) will undoubtedly add richness and texture to the picture, none of it should displace the central figure, Jesus, and the central idea, salvation.'[20]

You don't get this doctrine of blood atonement in Matthew's Gospel. You do get the proclamation of the coming, even imminent Kingdom. You *will* find the doctrine of Christ's role as an atoning sacrifice in Paul's epistles, and that is why Thompson suggests that Matthew's failure to mention it was '*possibly* more necessary' because of his audience. Nothing must stand in the way of the persisting emphasis on the radical solution to humankind's terrible plight, even if in this instance, the terrible plight is not mentioned by Matthew. His main criticism of alternative, more liberal views of salvation, is that 'they underplay the seriousness of sin and how it relates to salvation.'[21]

Thompson has spoken about God's holy wrath and judgment and anger against human sin, but has not explained what we are supposed to understand by the *seriousness* of sin. No one will argue with him about human failures and limitations or about the terrible things human beings often do to one another. But that is different to saying that *all* are in danger of God's judgment and condemnation unless they are 'saved' by Christ. Humans have also been good and noble, even heroic and self-sacrificing. If all of us have been 'lost' in original sin and deserving of God's terrible judgment, then it is difficult to understand where these positive virtues come from. Thompson stated categorically, that condemnation 'is exactly what we all deserve'. He ought to be put on the spot and asked to say clearly and without qualification, what he believes is the source or cause of humankind's 'fallen' nature. If it is not the fable of Eden and the 'Fall' of Adam and Eve, what is it? What has Christianity come up with since that explanation was rendered void of any historical or moral sense?

The third Australian theologian who expresses a more realistic and insightful commentary on 'the dwindling away of religion in more traditional form', is Scott Cowdell, the Canon Theologian of the Canberra and Goulburn Diocese of the Anglican Church of Australia. Cowdell is a realist who notes that while religion, in its traditional form is dwindling away, 'the Church doesn't always acknowledge it'. He tells us that the Anglican Church of Australia confronts these worrying trends with 'the official line that we simply need new skills and strategies'. That is obviously not working. His assessment of traditional Church life is bleak.

> The mainstream Churches, which in America are now regularly known as old-line churches, have lost their significant sociological function, apart from isolated community groups of increasingly elderly people, in which the world-transforming joy of the Gospel has typically settled into the warm afterglow of faith, often held together by a spirit of gentle nostalgia and ties of friendship ... if religion has any place it's a largely private one.[22]

Where Thompson boldly tells society it is sinful and in danger of God's judgment and wrath and must turn to the Gospel for the only salvation available, Cowdell is much more appreciative of the seriously troubling challenges to faith, and more willing to admit that it will take more than simply preaching the Gospel and trusting God to enable people to respond. The 'faithful preaching' of the past does not provoke the same results today.

> We don't look to God anymore because few of us believe the old story anymore: that God pulls all the levers in the world, and will do so in our favour if we pray, pay and obey. The old Sunday school faith of 'all things bright and beautiful' is gone, since we now know from Charles Darwin how life evolved on earth through the long and violent struggle of 'nature red in tooth and claw', as Tennyson put it ... We're no longer at home in the world with God in the same way, and hence today's rush in some quarters for a comforting spirituality, and wish-fulfilling romantic fantasies, because for many the robust self-assertion or else the quiet resignation of atheism is too much for them. Many still cling to some sense of wonder or purpose, but cancer and retrenchment can soon put a stop to that.[23]

In theological terms he is singling out concepts such as God's 'sovereignty' and the 'efficacy of prayer', and a pre-scientific understanding of the world and nature and acknowledging that the old 'certainties' have been left behind. We might say they are like old jalopies stranded on the road, no longer able to transport people around because the spare parts that might make them operable, are no longer available. While other more contemporary and independent churches with their upbeat themes of success, wholeness, healing, prosperity and victory, cheerfully talk about the hope we have in Christ and the marvellous difference he makes in our lives, Cowdell understands how confidence in divine providence is undermined when 'bad things happen undeservingly to most of us in life, and really terrible things to many people, despite their prayers.'[24]

We have reason to wonder he suggests, why, given the incredible technologies that have transformed civilization today, 'God couldn't have built the cosmic machine a lot better'. The problem of evil, perhaps the biggest challenge for Christian theology, is frequently addressed by apologists trying to make sense of a world over which God is supposed to preside. In my own ministry, I know that this was always a primary concern and discomfort for most people in my congregations. Cowdell makes no attempt to smooth over the difficulties involved in this question but tells us that 'the standard answers I find unsatisfactory'. I drew my title for this chapter from his comments about the problem of evil.

> Either God has a plan that includes child murders and killer tsunamis, or else God is so bound to honour natural laws and human freedom that nothing can be expected from God in terms of actual outcomes. The first of these answers makes God a monster, and the second makes God a handbag—an accessory to life but not a major player in it.[25]

This is the sort of comment you would expect to read in a work by an atheist, though an atheist would suggest additional descriptions to Cowdell's 'either- or'. The comment itself reminds us that there are Christians who continue to think deeply about these issues and who genuinely struggle with the implications of their beliefs. Most are not convincing in their proposed resolution of the problem of evil. Os Guinness is an English theologian who has had a huge impact on the Christian apologetics scene for decades. In his book *Unspeakable: Facing Up to the Challenge of Evil,* he attempts to offset the problem of evil, with the 'problem' of goodness. This is not original to Guinness, since it is a recurring theme in Christian writings. 'Could it be that there is a mystery to goodness that is even deeper than the mystery of evil? ... It is often set off even more brilliantly in contrast with surrounding evil'.[26] This is supposed to make us think that instead of blaming God for allowing so much evil, human and natural, we should credit him for inspiring goodness. Guinness does not actually say that, but that is what is implied.

It always strikes non-believers as odd and objectionable, that God should never be given the credit for any evil in the world, but must always be given the credit for the good. The idea that goodness might just be a natural expression of human nature that constantly battles with other, less commendable traits, and not something which God's 'Holy Spirit' generates in us, never occurs to those who must constantly be defending the ways of God. Guinness is right to say that faith should not be resorted to as a 'crutch because reason has stumbled', but goes to on recommend that we 'acknowledge that reason, in its long, arduous search, has come up short and that where it has stopped it has pointed beyond itself to answers that only faith can fulfil. In the face of the horror of the unspeakable, only such faith can provide the best truths to come to terms with evil'.[27] This is an unintelligible statement filled with unsupportable assumptions.

Where has reason come 'short' and where has it 'stopped' in its 'long arduous search'? Was it in its discovery of the true nature of the cosmos or in Darwin's discovery of the origins of all biological life on Earth? Was it in the constant war waged against disease and other causes of human suffering? Where in this arduous search, has it stopped and 'pointed beyond itself to answers that only faith can fulfil'? What answers has faith provided for the benefit of humankind and its chances of survival in the past five hundred years? Reason may stumble at times, but it continues to be our only hope for improvement, progress, the alleviation of suffering and the guarantee of future beneficial discoveries. Is it not, by contrast, faith which has stumbled and stopped? Isn't that the reason for the 'widespread intellectual doubts about Christian belief' that Cowdell acknowledges in his article?

After highlighting the problem of evil that continues to challenge Christian faith, Cowdell states that 'a related question is the suffering Jesus'. He seems to distance himself from the way this suffering has been understood throughout history 'as necessary to ward off the wrath of God' and credits belief in this punishing God' exercising 'naked sovereignty' over the world, as having 'played a part in alienating Christianity from modern people'.[28] Then he adds that another substantial challenge to faith is religious pluralism, 'the widespread contemporary experience that people of goodwill and compassion are all around us yet they profess no religious belief. A God who demands strict denominational allegiance simply doesn't compute anymore.'

Not only has Christianity failed to maintain any credible explanation for the origin of evil and human 'lostness', now it is confronted with widespread goodwill and compassion from people of *no religious belief.* Cowdell confesses that 'Few of us believe the old story anymore.' He is alluding to the traditional Christian explanations for human origins, nature and need for redemption. The 'old story' has long been replaced by a more compelling, self-evident one. So while conservative Christians like Sydney Anglicans still appeal to the old story to justify their Gospel account of salvation, and while liberal Christians qualify the old story to such an extent that it becomes unrecognisable, even meaningless, secularists and atheists write about goodness and morality, the goodwill and compassion of the non-religious millions.

A.C. Grayling has written *What is Good? The Search for the Best Way to Live,* Sam Harris has written *The Moral Landscape: How Science can Determine Human Values,* Greg Epstein, *Good without God: What a Billion Nonreligious People Do Believe,* Phil Zuckerman, *Living the Secular Life,* Eric Maisel, *The Atheist's Way: Living Well Without Gods,* and Stephen Pinker, *The Better Angels of our Nature.* It is these secular works that are promoting, not a new story, but rather the story that was there from the beginning, which has persisted through the ages. That story tells the real truth about human nature and human potential and it is a story that science and reason, rather than faith and superstition, continue to verify. As I re-read works of Christian theology and apologetics, I look for the conclusions they draw from the acknowledged challenges to faith.

> Addressing these challenges to belief, as theologians like me regularly do, is still not going to fix the problem that Christianity has lost its imaginative credibility, its sense of connecting us with the beating heart of life in the world as we know it … . I hope that I give deep and searching answers in my preaching, teaching and writing to these big questions, but that alone won't bring people back to the Church. Ideas alone won't help them across the significant cultural abyss that separates them from coming to Church every Sunday.[29]

What will help? The answer is not, as the official line of the Church suggested earlier, 'new skills and strategies', for those things belong to the world of the market and business management and not the world that is supposed to construct a bridge between Earth and Heaven. Nor does Cowdell believe it helps all that much to change patterns of worship—more guitars, de-emphasis on doctrine and sacraments and traditions. What then? 'Thankfully we can leave this to God to some extent.'[30] That's faith speaking. It is a faith which is 'the assurance of things hoped for, the conviction of things not seen' (Hebrews 11:1). It is admirable, but somewhat sad. Is it what Cowdell meant at the beginning of his article when he wrote that 'the real problems are programmatic reluctance and a widespread culture of depression'?[31]

When I was a younger minister there was much excited talk of some new 'revival' that would sweep the land, perhaps even the world, bringing thousands if not millions to Christ and reviving the fortunes of the Church. The days of mass crusades are definitely over and the hope of revival—historically thought to be a miraculous work of the Holy Spirit sweeping through a particular society or nation—seems to have faded away. There are plenty of Pentecostal-Charismatic independent churches where 'revival' is experienced locally and frequently, but if actual experience is any guide, the currency of the word has been greatly devalued. It is probably even less credible than their constant reports of miracles.

Scott Cowdell appears to remain in a state of patient waiting upon God. He does not presume to say what the answers to the challenges to faith are, only what they are not. And after expressing a willingness, to leave the matter in God's hands, he writes that 'Time will tell if this cultural decline of Christianity is in fact a complete rout, or rather a purifying transformation. Perhaps Christianity is downsizing to a more appropriately sized-home in the modern world. I certainly think so.'[32] But if he is right and Christianity is 'downsizing', what does that mean for its competitors? Islam is not downsizing. Some predict it will surpass Christianity in a decade or two. Hinduism, by virtue of geography and culture is not downsizing, and while Buddhism is in decline in some parts of the world, it seems to be gaining appeal, at least in the West.

Is Allah the dominant God of the future? Will Krishna surpass Christ as the object of human devotion and worship? Will enlightenment burst upon the world through the teachings of the Buddha? According to Buddhist tradition and the prediction of Buddha himself, a future Buddha called Maitreya will appear on Earth, achieve complete enlightenment, and teach the pure *dharma,* the natural law which upholds or supports the way of truth and enlightenment, to everyone. He is supposed to come at a future time when the dharma will have almost been forgotten by the world. What if Maitreya shows up before Christ's hoped for second-coming? If Christianity is in decline now, how will it not be even less relevant in any down-sizing exercise?

Like Tom Frame, Cowdell remains persuaded because of 'the Church's stubborn focus on Jesus: that there is a God who undergirds a world of wonder and belonging, and who holds us in God's loving arms despite the terrors of life'. What remains true for him is 'that word and sacrament, preaching, and the often difficult struggle of sticking together in the Church', for those are the things that still contribute to 'conversion and humanisation.'[33] It is a noble sentiment, but surely it is precisely that 'word', sacrament and preaching that sounds and appears less and less relevant or realistic to most people today and which persuades so many hundreds of thousands of Christians every year *not* to stick together in the Church, but to leave it without regret. And if there is 'a God who undergirds a world of wonder and belonging, and who holds us in (his) loving arms despite the terrors of life', then he will have to give us some more convincing reason to believe in his existence. Meanwhile, he remains invisible, silent and inert. In my final chapter, I relate in a more personal way, why I have been unable and unwilling to stick with the Church, and why I have made the journey from faith to humanism.

The Man Behind the Veil

Truth is grey, and deceit is full of splendour.

–Abraham Joshua Heschel

Most of us who have made the journey from religion to humanism have often lived several lives as someone else—a Christian, a Muslim, a Mormon etc., The world of religion is a bewildering galaxy of differing stars. Mormonism, Christianity and Judaism have been the three most formative influences in my own life. I remain a student of Mormonism because it is a unique example of a religion which was born and evolved, flourishing to become a minor world religion in relatively recent times. It took 117 years, from its establishment in New York State in 1830 until 1947, for the Church to grow from the initial six members to one million. Since then, over the last 69 years, it has grown to fifteen million. I have already made several references to Mormonism in the previous chapters, but want to discuss part of my personal experience of the religion here in this chapter as a means of illustrating my overall theme about the falsity of all religion.

After my family immigrated to Australia from Scotland in 1957, my parents continued to send me to Sunday school, usually the Church of England, as it was known before 1977 (when it became the Anglican Church of Australia). It was while attending high school l between 1960 and 1964 that I was in earnest about religion. A neighbour used to talk with me about religion when I went in to visit her in her flat next to ours. She introduced me to the Christadelphians whose focus on the end-time and the Second Coming of Christ always fascinated me. Then one day she involved me in a visit from two young American Mormon missionary elders, Elder Kai Cedar and Elder Gerald Langton. That visit was to change my life for years to come.

Barely fourteen, I sat and listened to those young men with American accents and was immediately struck by their sincerity, simplicity and confidence. The fact that I had been seeking for 'something' since the age of twelve, seemed to have prepared me for that afternoon meeting. I hadn't found it at Sunday school or in Scripture periods at school, but that day I knew I had found it. They told me how the 'true' Church of Jesus Christ had been restored to the earth in these latter days through a modern prophet called Joseph Smith. When he had his first vision of God and Jesus in 1820, he wasn't much older than I was when I first heard about him. I had never understood the Trinity, but Joseph Smith's First Vision told me that there was no such thing. God the father was God and Jesus was his Son and there were simply two of them—as I had suspected all along! Suddenly, convincingly, the elders from Utah helped me to see the truth about God in a way that satisfied my young and impressionable mind.

Within weeks I had read the Book of Mormon and wanted to be baptised a member of the Church of Jesus Christ of Latter-day Saints (Mormon Church). Today as the father of two sons of my own, and now three grandchildren, I can appreciate the alarm and consternation this announcement caused my bewildered parents. The idea of one of my boys adopting an alien religion at the tender age of fourteen would have caused me some concern too. But back in 1960-61, I felt only hurt and confusion at my parents, particularly my mother's, negative response. Did I know what I was doing, she asked? Hadn't I already been baptised as a baby? Who were these Mormons anyway? An American cult, a threat to the Christian churches. The fact that my parents were not themselves church-goers, made me angry that they should be opposing my religious conscience and choice.

Now that I am much older, I can understand their natural desire to protect me and keep me on a 'normal' path. After all, the Mormon Church in Australia in 1960 was still a relatively unknown and unorthodox religious movement with a membership of about 10,000. Today it claims a membership of about 140,000 in 208 'wards' or churches and has built five temples in Australian capital cities, though Australian Bureau of Statistics suggests that the actual membership may be less than 50% of that figure because the Church is reluctant to remove the names of 'inactive' members. On December 17, 1961 at the age of fourteen years and seven months I was baptised and confirmed a member of the Mormon Church, at the Greenwich, Sydney chapel. With great enthusiasm and a new sense of purpose I sang the hymns of Zion.

> The morning breaks, the shadows flee;
> Lo, Zion's standard is unfurled!
> The dawning of a brighter day,
> Majestic rises on the world.
> The clouds of error disappear,
> Before the rays of truth divine;
> The glory bursting from afar,
> Wide o'er the nations soon will shine.[1]

I could not have known then, that being a Mormon would one day take me to the beautiful islands of Hawaii and the United States mainland, that my mother would be bewildered and disappointed when I finally *left* the Mormon Church in 1970, or that I would become a well-known anti-Mormon speaker in Sydney in the late 70's, 80's and 90's. But back in 1961, before colour television, before covered connecting walkways to aircraft at Australian airports and before the completion of Sydney's first 'sky-scraper', the AMP building at Circular Quay, life was all before me and Mormonism was my passion and future.

After finishing high school I worked for two years in order to save money to go to university overseas and finally in 1967, at the age of 20, said goodbye to my family and flew out of Sydney bound for Honolulu, Hawaii and further up the coast, to the Church College of Hawaii (CCH). Laie is a small university town, the home of the Hawaii Campus of the Brigham Young University, the largest, privately-owned university in the United States. When I enrolled in 1967, after spending five years as a convert to Mormonism in Sydney, it was simply called the Church College of Hawaii, a liberal arts college. Over four years I made many wonderful friends, shared rich and memorable experiences, devoted myself to my studies and my Mormon culture and regularly kept in touch with my family at home in Australia.

Baptism is a primary 'ordinance' that admits a person into membership of the Mormon Church, but sooner or later every Mormon must go to the Temple (not a normal meeting house or chapel) and receive the 'higher ordinances' of the Gospel. The township of Laie is also home to one of Hawaii's most visited tourist attractions, the Hawaii Temple of the Church of Jesus Christ of Latter-day Saints (built in 1919), sometimes known as the 'Taj Mahal of the Pacific'. Well, not quite. I served as a guide for tourist groups on the grounds of the Temple when I was not in classes or working off my student loan. My own initiation into the higher ordinances of the Gospel, called the *Endowment*, took place in the Hawaii Temple on the sixth of December 1967. That was the day when I was ushered into the presence of God. During that lengthy ceremony I swore on pain of death, never to reveal the secrets of the priesthood revealed to me.

Temples or 'Houses of the Lord' as Mormons call them, are unique spiritual edifices in which sacred religious ordinances for both the living and the dead are performed. They are multi-million dollar structures open only to faithful Mormons who have been judged worthy to enter their astonishingly beautiful interiors. Mormons do so in order to enhance provisions for their personal salvation and life in the hereafter. Temples are closed to the non-Mormon public and even those Mormons who enter them swear on pain of death never to reveal what they hear and see inside the Temple. Well at least they did when I went through in 1967. Since then the Church has revised its Temple ritual several times and removed some of the more disturbing and contentious elements. And as far as secrecy is concerned, there have been so many defections from the Mormon faith and so many exposes of the Temple ritual, that it no longer remains much of a secret.

My own 'Endowment' visit was to be the first of a number of visits to the Temple. Later, on a number of occasions, I was submerged in a baptistery or font resting on the backs of twelve carved marble oxen, acting as proxy in baptism for dozens of deceased persons. Baptisms for the dead—several million are performed every year in 144 operating temples throughout the world, with 14 more under construction—constitute the major work of the Temple.

The *Endowment* is a kind of rite of passage ceremony which teaches truths about the meaning of life on earth and provides candidates with information for their eventual passage into eternity. Since Mormons are not allowed to talk about the details of the ceremony outside the Temple, I did not know quite what to expect. I had read statements like that made by two Mormon writers, McConkie and Millet, that 'some experiences are ineffable, so tremendously glorious that they defy human expression or description.'[2] In hindsight, the actual experience did not quite live up to the expectation, but it was one of the more remarkable experiences of my life. It isn't necessary for me to go into all the details here, except to say that the ceremony represents a symbolic journey through life from creation to one's own death and at its conclusion, an entry into heaven or the Celestial Kingdom. It is that conclusion I want to comment on.

After proceeding through a number of splendidly-designed rooms with vast, illustrative murals, candidates come at last to the white Veil of the Temple. With other members of my group I was shown the veil and the sacred marks on it which correspond with those on the special Temple undergarments which covered our bodies. We were told that the ceremony would culminate, like our mortal lives, with our passing through the Veil into the grandest room of the Temple—the Celestial Room representing Heaven. Before being permitted passage through the veil, we were required to feed back all the 'signs', 'tokens', and 'passwords' that we had been shown during our initiation, to a 'worker' behind the Veil who represented God, our Heavenly Father. The whole purpose of the Endowment ceremony is essentially to provide Mormons with these signs and tokens which are mainly special Masonic-like handgrips.

The worker behind the Veil asked particular questions of us and presented his hand through slits in the Veil so as to receive the proper responses. One further piece of information is required in order to complete the symbolic journey. It is the name of the 'Second Token of the Aaronic Priesthood', the Patriarchal Grip or 'Sure Sign of the Nail.' It is given by the 'Lord' himself, but only 'upon the Five Points of Fellowship through the Veil.' Though only in my twentieth year, I can still remember getting my body into place on one side of the Veil so that it aligned properly with the worker on the other side. I reached for the hand which had poked through the slit and held it firmly while pushing my left hand and arm through another opening in the Veil so as to touch the back of the 'Lord' on the other side. He did the same thing, so that we ended up in a kind of embrace with only the curtain between us. Once our legs made contact in the knee-to-knee position, I was ready to receive the 'name' of the Token. Having given all the signs asked of me by continuing to clutch the hand of the 'Lord', I was drawn through the Veil into the Celestial Room.

This is always the most lavishly furnished of all the great rooms in the Temple, its expensive furniture and decor designed to suggest our heavenly mansions and rewards. They are a bit like the entrance foyer of an especially luxurious Marriot Hotel (John Willard Marriot Jr., son of the founder and present CEO, is a devout Mormon). As each of us was filtered through the veil in silence, we stood for a while in the central room of the Temple. I don't quite remember what I expected to happen then, but apart from being able to briefly occupy the room itself, nothing else follows. That's it. No prayers, singing, kneeling or postures of worship of any kind. You are simply informed that the ceremony has been completed and that you are to return to the change rooms, put on your street clothes and leave the Temple. For me it meant a quick change and then a brisk walk across the lawns and fields between the Temple and the University campus where I re-entered my dormitory.

Only a peculiarly Mormon conception of God as a glorified man who has himself progressed through aeons of time and similar ordinances of salvation, would encourage people to believe that the Endowment is a necessary requirement for future glory or complete salvation. Mormonism *does* believe in the atoning sacrifice of Christ for the forgiveness of sins, but more is required if a person is going to inherit the highest heaven hereafter. That 'more' is the 'laws and ordinances' of the Mormon Gospel, especially those of the Temple. Like Christianity telling Judaism that 'mere forgiveness' through repentance is not enough because the atoning blood of Christ is also required, Mormonism tells Christianity, that simply believing in Jesus is not enough, there are other additional requirements for salvation.

There is no doubt that the Temple's symbolic journey through time to eternity, helps Mormons to understand their place in the great scheme of things. It helps them make contact with the world beyond and just as a foreign embassy is regarded as a portion of its nation's sovereign domain or territory, so the Temple is already the presence of heaven on earth. I certainly subscribed then to the belief that God, the Supreme Being, provided his 'true' Church on earth with such sacred ordinances for the salvation of his people. And though within a few years I would abandon that Church and its unorthodox God, it would be many more years before

I would abandon the idea of God altogether. In 2013, I returned to Hawaii with my wife Rhonda for a holiday and we visited the Temple grounds in Laie. It was the first time in forty-four years that I had seen the place. It did stir some real, emotional impressions, for the place will always embody a unique and formative experience in my life. Nevertheless, I have never had any regrets or mental reservations about leaving Mormonism.

The idea of encountering God or someone pretty much like him behind a veil also appears in L. Frank Baum's classic American fairy-tale, *The Wonderful Wizard of Oz*. When Dorothy and her companions, the Tinman, the Lion and the Scarecrow finally reach their destination at the end of the Yellow Brick Road, they come to the Emerald City and are anxious to meet with the Great Wizard himself. There in the glistening city, they are ushered into the Palace of Oz and into his throne room. Like the Celestial Room in Mormon Temples, the Throne Room is bright and splendid and filled with light. The Wizard, like the God in the Mormon Temple, is not actually seen—though he does project a terrible visage—but speaks from behind a veil. When Dorothy, seeing no one, only hearing the voice, asks him where he is, he answers, 'I am everywhere, but to the eyes of common mortals I am invisible,'[3] which sounds like the familiar description of the Biblical God.

This impressive and frightening confrontation comes to a head when Dorothy's little dog Toto jumps in alarm at the sound of the Wizard's voice and tips over the curtain or screen that stands in the room. As Dorothy and her friends look this way and that, they are astonished to see a little old man standing where the screen had been. When they ask him who he is, he replies that he is Oz, the Great and Terrible. In their surprise and dismay they exclaim what they each thought Oz was—a great head (Dorothy), a lovely lady (Scarecrow), a terrible beast (Tin Woodman) and a ball of fire (the lion). It is then that the Wizard confesses that he has 'been making believe' and that he is just 'a common man.'[4]

In fact he is a ventriloquist from Omaha, Nebraska who, tired of his work in a circus became a balloonist. One day he travelled above the clouds and landed in a green and beautiful country. The people there thought he was a wizard, so they built a palace for him and named their city, Emerald City. The Wizard made its inhabitants wear green-tinted glasses so that they would believe the city was indeed an Emerald city. He explained this as an effort to protect their eyes from the 'brightness and glory' of the city. The effect was to make everything appear green when it was, in fact, 'no more green than any other city.'

Towards the end of Baum's story, later made into a famous film starring Judy Garland, the Wizard asks Dorothy and her friends not to tell the people what they have learned on the condition that he would show Dorothy how to get back to Kansas. She went along with this arrangement, even though she ended up calling him 'The Great and Terrible Humbug.' Baum of course, was not a believer. Though he dabbled in Theosophy, he did not believe that God was any more real than the Wizard of Oz. His tale has Dorothy's characters realizing that the qualities they seek to be fulfilled and happy, are within themselves and were never going to be provided by some benevolent, all-powerful, outside power or Wizard (God).

The man behind the veil in that Temple in Hawaii was only playing the part of God, representing God for the purpose of facilitating a sacred ritual. The man behind the curtain in *The Wonderful Wizard of Oz* was pretending to be a godlike figure, a great wizard in order to rule benevolently over the people whose land he had stumbled upon. Joseph Smith (1805-1844), founder of the Mormon religion, once dared his followers to consider his radical view of God. He spoke of God 'enthroned in yonder heavens … as a man like unto one of yourselves.' He said that if he could tear away the veil that hides God from human eyes and understanding then people would 'see him in all the person, image and very form as a man; for Adam was created in the very fashion and image of God'.[5] Though the contemporary

Mormon church has back-peddled from such bold statements today, they remain part of the very foundation of Mormonism. How great an edifice may be raised on the foundations of such grand illusions.

In recent years my personal conviction has been that a growing number of people suspect that *God* is the man behind the screen or veil. They may have once believed in him as Dorothy and her fellow travelers did in their own imaginative ways. Perhaps he is not to them a great and imposing head, a lovely lady, a terrible beast or a ball of fire. They have their own ideas and images of him, most of which are not helped by the incomprehensible creeds of the Church which include such baffling teachings as the Trinity. In their disillusionment they may have been angry with the object of their one-time devotion and ended up calling him as Dorothy did, 'the Great and Terrible Humbug'. Or else devotion may have faded to indifference with the growing instinct that claims for God's existence and revealed word are simply not credible; that many of the things religious friends challenged them to accept, are really delusions. For these people, the collapse of the veil reveals not so much a little old man, a human projection of a wondrous being, but no one and nothing at all. There simply is no Wizard of Oz, no Lord God Almighty.

It was while completing my studies for my B.A. and Teacher's Certificate in Hawaii, that I became increasingly disillusioned with the origins and history of Mormonism and the character of its founder, Joseph Smith. After a great deal of soul-searching and personal anguish, I stopped believing in the Mormon faith as the result of discovering what I believed to be real Christianity in the pages of the New Testament. For this 'apostasy' I was dealt with in a formal trial of excommunication in 1969. I was in my final period of studies, was editor of the College newspaper, *Ke Alaka'i*, a representative on the Student Honour Council, and a student in History, president of the Xi Delta Chapter of the History Honour Society, Phi Alpha Theta. It proved to be a difficult last year and a lot was at stake.

Mormonism had appeared in the beginning, to be that self-evident truth for all people. That was until I discovered the questionable nature of its origins and the way in which the whole complex, evolving structure had been put together. It was before I discovered that the Book of Mormon was not a true record of the peoples of ancient America, that its cities and civilizations had never existed on the American continent. And it was before I stopped believing that the sacred (and secret) rites of the Temple were really 'avenues to exaltation, symbols of a love divine', and came to see the Temple as yet another exclusive institution, promising salvation only to the initiated, to those who had received its sacred ordinances as I had in Hawaii. Mormonism had given me some of the happiest and most fulfilling years of my young life, but in the end, I forsook the magnificent illusion.

Mormonism was the faith of my youth and I had been devoted to it heart and soul. It still exerts something of an emotional, though totally irrational influence over me as one would expect from the most impressionable years of life. That could be said about my later experiences of Christianity and Judaism as well. The discovery of its essential falsehood and the loss of all the certainties it gave me—worldview, Joseph Smith as a prophet, newly revealed scriptures, the institution of the temple and priesthood, the divinely-established community or church—proved an immense loss. You move on of course, but the experience leaves its mark. It may even be that that initial experience of disillusionment and loss—itself a 'revelation'—led me ultimately to question the faith that replaced it.

The loss of course was compensated by a conversion to mainstream Christianity, but the critical faculties and criteria which led me to question and doubt and ultimately disown Mormonism, continued with me as a Christian. I could not help but apply them to some aspects of Christianity as well. The sword of truth truly is two-edged. It does cut both ways. So that long after leaving Mormonism I found myself asking questions about the Old and New Testaments and the evolution of Hebrew faith, questions that I once asked only of the Book of Mormon. As Mark Twain said: 'The easy confidence with which I know another man's religion is folly teaches me to suspect that my own is also'.

Cicero (106-43 BCE), the great Roman orator and statesman in his book *The Nature of the Gods,* has one of his characters, Cota, complain 'that he was quite happy to take his religion on trust from tradition, *but the more it is defended by argument, the more doubtful it becomes*'. And at the end of Book III, Section XXXIX, Cicero adds, that while he is not intent on destroying belief in the gods, he has wanted 'but merely to show what an obscure point it is, and with what difficulties an explanation of it is attended'.[6] That sentiment certainly proved true for me.

I have always had a need to know that whatever I believed the truth to be, it had to be the truth for *everyone*, not just for some, and that everyone had to have equal access to it. It had to be a self-evident truth, not some obscure or exclusive philosophy that the majority might fail to grasp. That conviction always led me to take the apologist's approach as the most effective means of evangelism. Give people *reasons* to believe what they ought to believe, show them that God's truth has a rational basis—despite being ultimately beyond the ken of mortal minds—and that he has provided evidence of his truth, and they will not be disappointed if they are honestly seeking.

Reflecting on the past and remembering several spiritual experiences in Mormonism and Catholicism—stirrings of the heart, dreams, voices, answered prayer etc., it seems to me that settled conviction cannot be based on subjective experiences, however impressive, for each appears to validate its own context (Mormonism, Catholicism) and cannot be held to if it contradicts reason and common sense. There were probably good psychological reasons for my 'spiritual' experiences, but they provide no real evidence for a supernatural realm. My studies of World Religions amply demonstrates that millions of people hold to their differing faith systems, not because of rational arguments or evidence, but because of personal experiences, feelings, emotions, psychological states. As others have said, all these different religions can't all be right, but they could all be wrong.

My friend, professor Malcolm Jeeves of St. Andrews, Scotland, wrote in his book, *Neuroscience Psychology and Religion: Illusions, Delusions and Realities about Human Nature:*

> Our human lives with our beliefs and hopes, are both embodied in our physical brains and embedded in our societies and cultures, whether we as individuals happen to be religious or not. Our scientific understanding of human nature is advancing rapidly. In all likelihood, science will begin to decipher the operation of some of our most cherished religious experiences, such as sudden or 'miraculous' conversions or healings. Religious beliefs, in general, and Christian faith in particular, must prepare for that day.[7]

I wrote to Malcolm asking him to spell out the implications of that last sentence, implications which I think are all too clear. He has his own way of dealing with those implications and remains a committed Christian, but I think the rapidly developing field of neuroscience is another 'Toto' pulling away the veil and exposing the Wizard. Popular writers like Michael Shermer and Sam Harris, himself a neuroscientist, have written helpfully on this subject. The neurologist Kevin Nelson seems to pick up where Jeeves leaves off.

> The brain pathways used during 'natural' spiritual experiences are the same pathways used by spiritual drugs, indistinguishable from otherwise genuine religious conversions, transforming lives long after the drug is flushed clear from the body. Clinical neurology tells us these are the same pathways distorted by some diseases of the brain that produce disorders fitting criteria for religious experience. . . We have strong indications that much of our spirituality arises from arousal, limbic, and reward systems that evolved long before structures made the brain capable of language and reasoning. Neurologically, mystical feelings may not be so much beyond language as *before* language.

And then, after suggesting evidences that other primates, including Neanderthals had mystical feelings and a sense of the afterlife, Nelson concludes ...

These are challenging ideas. Our spiritual nature may not be the last bastion of human specialness, a particularly uncomfortable thought as advances in cosmology are magnifying our smallness and seeming insignificance in the face of a massive and mechanical universe.[8]

One of America's great humanist poets was Walt Whitman. I discovered him years ago in my first brush with humanism by first reading his *Leaves of Grass*. One passage in particular seems relevant here:

> Gradually, inevitably, came the unavoidable conclusion:
> A vague mist hanging 'round half the pages:
> (Sometimes how strange and clear to the soul,
> That all these solid things are indeed but apparitions,
> concept, non-realities).
>
> Walt Whitman, *Apparitions* from 'Leaves of Grass'.

What I have come to discover, what *I* have come to discover (I realise many people will not agree with me), is that 'all these solid things', particularly the idea of God, are indeed 'apparitions.' And when I talk about God, I mean the traditional idea of the God of the Jews and Christians. I do not know what other kinds of supreme beings or super-intelligences or life-forces might exist in the Universe—if any. It may well be that we are alone. Alone or not we struggle to understand what *is*, what our minds and experiences teach us.

In my last year of ministry I led a discussion at church in the fortnightly *Insight Hour* on 'Struggles and Doubts' based on several texts seeking to analyse why young people and evangelicals in general, continue to leave the church in great numbers. The Bible study topic which I thought would be helpful and faith-building, simply raised numerous issues which remained unresolved. Of course there are many sociological and historical reasons for the Church's decline, at least in the West, but I think it is more helpful to see that it is the actual *teachings* of Christianity which many find harder to accept. Certainly that was true for me.

Some recent Evangelical publications are focusing on what they are conceding is a massive decrease in evangelical influence politically, economically, culturally and financially. In *The Great Evangelical Recession,* John S. Dickerson reports that '260,000 evangelical young people walk away from Christianity each year. Of that number 35% will find their way back and 65% do not find their way back.' Dickerson asks why they are leaving and answers candidly, 'They don't believe anymore.' I find that fascinating because that is the *one* reason evangelicals usually don't deal with very well. Dickerson notes that the Church is losing 2.6 million people per decade and that is only from one generation. 'The fastest growing subcultures in the United States express a militant antagonism against Christians who take the Bible seriously.'[9]

From a Christian point of view such serious decline is usually seen as evidence of increasing 'secularism' (a dirty word) or 'Godlessness' in the 'last days'. Most Evangelical analysts seem incapable of seeing that the Christian faith itself may simply be incomprehensible or incoherent to growing numbers of people. At least Dickerson seems willing to consider that. Speaking about the trend of decline in the Church, he says that 'The megatrend reveals a trajectory of massive regression—far larger than the simple sum of the parts.'[10] His book has been written to address the challenge of this downward trend and suggest 'how much altitude can we lose before crashing?' Who exactly is he talking about?

> We're talking about churches and individuals who believe a salvation-by-faith-alone 'gospel.' We're talking about American Christians who believe the Bible is God's Word, that it is without error, and that Jesus is the only way to salvation and to God. This broad group includes a wide variety: Pentecostals, Baptists, charismatics, fundamentalists, those who believe you can lose your salvation, those who believe you can't, Calvinistic, non-Calvinistic, and so forth. But all of these churches believe Jesus is the only way to God, and that Scripture is God's authoritative Word.[11]

Interestingly, for those who think that Evangelicals in America are numerically large and influential, Dickerson tells us that independent analysts have concluded that Evangelicalism is about one-fourth of its claimed size. This is similar to sociologists of religion who have already said that the statistics of the Mormon Church may be exaggerating the actual, active membership by 40 to 50%. Dickerson agrees with the analysts, despite the fact that he is still hopeful for the Christian future. 'We're going to see a massive discrepancy between the number of Americans who claim to be born again and the experts' count of evangelicals. The reason for the discrepancy is simple: A lot of Americans *say* they're born again, but when prodded, they do not believe what evangelical Christians believe.'[12] It could be argued of course, that Christianity is much larger than its Evangelical expression, which has usually been healthier than the alternative traditions like Orthodoxy or Liberal Christianity. Yet even in those communities there are many who express disagreement with central tenets and practices of their faith.

In our studies together at church and in the first session or Introduction to *Struggles and Doubts,* I was struck, not so much by the fact that the group were anxious to discuss such issues and quite able to volunteer their own lists of troublesome, doubt-provoking topics, but the more unsettling observation that they really do not comprehend a lot of the beliefs or doctrines of the Church, and are incapable of articulating how they think about them. Retreating to the confines of a 'simple' faith may terminate struggles and stifle doubt, but it also imprisons the soul with a false comfort.

The Scottish minister and New Testament scholar William Barclay, once wrote that: 'By and large the Church has been afraid to introduce the ordinary man to the results of biblical scholarship and the new thought. They have had the feeling that the people will not stand it. It is in fact what the people are crying out for.' He then went on to relate experiences of how other ministers he had known had shared some of these difficulties with their congregations and how, surprisingly, individuals had responded with relief and appreciation, because they confessed that they themselves had drawn these same conclusions.

Barclay relates how in his books and on air he tried to share the results of modern scholarship and as a result, received angry letters and accusations of his being a destroyer of the faith and a heretic. But others wrote and expressed their appreciation. He concluded: 'The Church will never communicate until it is honest, until ministers stop forgetting in the pulpit all that they have learned in the classroom, until in courage and in honesty and in sincerity they respect the people to whom they preach, and treat them as thinking adults and not as children who cannot stand the truth.'[13]

Barclay is someone I always readily identified with, though merely mentioning his name in the Presbyterian circles in which I ministered, provoked suspicion and concern. Barclay was regarded, particularly by Presbyterians in Australia, as a notorious liberal. While I had from time to time, shared challenging issues with the congregation, I did not think it was my job to share with them the enormity of the troublesome issues presently in existence. It seemed neither wise nor necessary. What would be the point? Most people usually believe what they want to believe and it seldom has much to do with rational arguments. Such restraint became increasingly difficult for me in the last year or so when my own doubts were increasing exponentially.

One of the things we learn in life is that truth is stranger and more elusive than we may have thought or wanted to believe. I think of all the time and energy and passion that occupied my mind and the minds of others in years past and now conclude that most of it was useless and unprofitable. When I first started theological college in the late 70's and early 80's, Baptists were obsessed with the issue of the 'Inerrancy of Scripture'. Volumes were written and read, debates seemed endless. Churches were split. Then there was the Creation-Evolution issue which still rages in some places, but is largely left behind by more scientifically-enlightened Christians. Beyond that, in my Presbyterian days, I encountered the debate about the ordination of women to the ministry, arguing the case *for* at a local, regional, state and national level within the institutional Presbyterian Church of Australia. There I was plainly in a minority, though my congregations have always supported me in this. Debate still flares up as I mentioned in previous chapters, over the nature of the atonement and the person of Christ.

In the end, what did all that controversy and debate, all of it in-house stuff achieve? The Bible is not inerrant. Writers like Paul were creatures of their time and culture. What they wrote about women or redemption or anything else was the product of their own mind and not the revelation of any god. Once that is admitted, then all the torturous debates about the interpretation of Scripture become unnecessary, even futile. The Bible, both Old and New Testaments is far more flawed and humanly-inspired than I could have imagined before. And as far as the Creation-Evolution debate is concerned, Creationists are now a thoroughly discredited species. All the Earth sciences clearly demonstrate the truth of Evolution with all its attendant implications for anthropology and the doctrines of sin and the Fall. I never now give a second thought to the contentious issue of women in ministry, since the whole idea of priesthood, authority and established ministry is quite alien to me, and I simply do not accept what one or two verses of Scripture say about women. The Bible and religion generally have a lot to answer for in their discrimination against half the human race.

As far as the person of Jesus is concerned, I continue to 'believe' in him, not as God incarnate or as saviour and redeemer, but as a true son of Israel, a thoroughly Jewish prophetic voice and one whose central message was not himself, but rather the imminent arrival of the Kingdom of his Father and his God. But that day has not yet arrived and redemption has not yet come to the world. I now believe that it never will in the sense that Jesus and the prophets spoke of—even Jesus was mistaken—but that our survival and flourishing as a species depends entirely on ourselves, there being no external powers or saviours or gods to help us.

I lament the fact that too many years of my life have also been concerned with Reformed theology, at one time passionately defending Calvinism and then, after many years of disillusionment with it, seeing it as an incoherent, reprehensible theology, one of the worst devised by the human mind. All that energy and time spent in vain. These are now matters of little importance, at least to me, though obviously, they continue to be to others. One of the surprises of life is that it can often take a long time to understand the forces that have shaped our lives. Merely studying other religions can take much time, but actually becoming involved in those other religions takes much more time and energy and passion. It has taken me to my sixty-eighth year. I haven't just studied other religious faiths, I have *been* a Presbyterian, a Mormon, a Roman Catholic, and almost a Jew.

It may well be that I am more critical of the Bible because I once learned to be critical of the Book of Mormon and the Book of Abraham. I see similar errors in both scriptures and am no more convinced by the explanations or excuses given for one as for the other. Many things about the Old and New Testament scriptures are questionable and in places, betray an all too human rather than divine influence. Liberal scholars have been aware of these for centuries, but conservative scholars continue to defend the problems. They often do so in the same ways that I know Mormon scholars have done with their scriptures and claims. These are problems for religion in general and not just for Christianity or Mormonism or Judaism in particular.

As the recent past has shown, I had two choices. Either remain a sceptical, liberal-minded Christian, hanging on to some kind of vague, but defensible spirituality, or abandon the religious enterprise altogether, as I once did. I chose the latter. Unlike the other religious periods of my life, my present state has not been difficult, nor has it increased my anxiety or fear of loss. If anything it has confirmed a state of mind I once experienced when I first considered the possibility that there was no God or supernatural reality. The conviction has grown steadily stronger and clearer.

'God is Plain to Them'?

If Christian theologians have no answer to the question of
the salvation of the greater part of mankind, they cannot be surprised
when people react again as they have done in the past:
Voltaire pouring out his scorn for the Church's
presumption in claiming to be the sole way of salvation ...

–Hans Kung

I sometimes feel guilty that as a Christian, particularly as a preacher, I made presumptuous statements about the spiritually defective state of nonbelievers. Most Christians reassure their own sense of being right by assuming that nonbelievers are being wilfully neglectful of their immortal souls and stubbornly disinterested in the things that matter most—eternal things. It was not enough to say that those outside of the Church were *ignorant* of the truth or even that they were *indifferent*. The New Testament made it clear that they were also personally culpable for deliberately suppressing the truth, a truth that was supposed to be self-evident. We could employ a favourite text of Paul's from the book of Romans to make this point.

> For the wrath of God is revealed from heaven against all ungodliness and wickedness of those who by their wickedness suppress the truth. For *what can be known about God is plain to them*, (emphasis mine)

> because God has shown it to them. Ever since the creation of the world his eternal power and divine nature, invisible though they are, have been understood and seen through the things he has made. So they are without excuse; for they knew God they did not honour him as God or give thanks to him, but they became futile in their thinking, and their senseless minds were darkened. Claiming to be wise, they became fools ... (Romans 1:18-22).

We used this verse so often to explain *why* people don't believe, that we seldom paused long enough to think how immensely unfair and grotesque such an assessment of human nature is. People who suppress a 'knowledge' of God are wicked. They are without excuse. They have 'senseless minds'. They are 'fools.' This assessment applies to everyone from Christopher Hitchens, a favourite target, to the otherwise perfectly normal and nice Mr. Jones living next door to you who has told you he isn't interested when you try to 'witness' to him or tell him about his need for Jesus. The first massive assumption of this text is that the existence of God 'is plain to them'. The ever-articulate Hitchens could always explain why such a thing was not plain to him, and millions of us agreed with him, while poor Mr. Jones doesn't really know why he doesn't believe in God.

If truth be told, he hasn't thought much about it and hasn't ever sensed any compelling reasons for believing such a thing. It's not plain to him either. Teaching groups of retired people through the courses offered by the 'University of the Third Age', I am also aware that many older people are very mentally inquisitive and eager to learn about other world religions and philosophies. Most of those same people have considered Christianity and concluded that it is not something they can believe in. Are they also 'senseless' and 'fools' and deserving of God's condemnation?

And as for Paul declaring that the existence of God has clearly been revealed 'through the things he has made', this may have been a reasonable argument in the First century, but it has not been at all persuasive for at least the last five centuries. All the dramatic and astonishing discoveries science has revealed about the nature and size of the Universe, have not left us with any clue to the existence of a god or gods. Many of the things God has allegedly made in nature are pretty horrible and cruel, as everyone since Darwin has come to know. Whether it is a *parasitoid* wasp—a revolting example much illustrated in atheist literature—invisible killer diseases that have created huge infant mortality rates in the past and still kill millions of all age-groups today, the world is so filled with things hostile to human life and survival that we cannot see God clearly in any of it.

Dinosaurs first appeared during the Triassic period, 231.4 million years ago, some considerable time before Adam and his Edenic paradise, and were the dominant vertebrates on Earth for over 100 million years. They were still around a mere 66 million years ago. Gazing in wonder at the ferocious nature of carnivores like the Tyrannosaurus Rex or the Velociraptor ('raptor'), both made terrifyingly real to us through Steven Spielberg's movie, *Jurassic Park*, it is very difficult to understand what we are supposed to understand about the nature of God by seeing these monsters. Mr. Jones may not know much about God, but he does know a bit about dinosaurs and he has probably heard of babies dying of various diseases.

Would preachers today or apologists for Paul, really claim that the clues to God's existence are clearly revealed in nature? They do continue to insist that we narrow our focus to the 'all things bright and beautiful, all creatures great and small', and ignore the ugly, the grotesque and the cruel, but not many Christians sing that old hymn today with any great sense of conviction. I used to think then and definitely do now, that we were too hard on our non-Christian neighbors and were always hard-pressed when people asked us for any real evidence for God's existence. A God who remains invisible, silent and apparently inert, is hard to explain or defend.

That difficulty in explaining God, however, did not stop us from placing the blame for irreligion squarely on the shoulders of our nonbelieving neighbours. Being a Christian, and I am sure it is the same if you are Muslim or something else, does affect the way you think about people, even people you love and admire. It is the old problem of assessing people on the basis of what they do or do not *believe*, rather than on what they essentially *are*. Christians are stuck with the belief yardstick in measuring themselves against others. Perhaps the following analogy explains what I am trying to say about people who don't believe in God—the 'unbelievers', the 'lost'. Let's call it the 'Loch Ness Monster Analogy'. Others have used the mystery of the Loch Ness Monster to make other points. I've put my own spin on it.

When I last saw Loch Ness in 2009, I did not see the monster. But then I wasn't looking for the monster, simply enjoying the day walking about Urquhart Castle on the banks of the famous Loch. Even as my wife and I looked out across the deep waters rippling in the wind and sparkling in the sunlight, we never gave a second thought to the monster. We were simply admiring the stunning natural beauty of that place. If for a moment we *had* thought of the monster, the moment quickly passed because while stories of its sighting are on the record in Scotland, most people don't take its existence seriously, so they don't spend any time either thinking about it or looking for it. At one point in the visit we walked down to the water's edge to get closer to the shore. If at that moment we had heard a roar and seen some turbulence breaking the surface of the water across the way, we might have momentarily thought about the monster, but more likely, would have looked and waited for some kind of natural explanation for the noise and the turbulence.

Isn't this a little like our life in the world in the absence of God? People move through the world, enjoying its natural beauty and rarely give a thought to the existence or presence of God. Not because they are godless in the sense of being willfully opposed to God or morally defective, but because *they have no reason to believe there is a God*. We know there are people who claim to have 'seen' God or heard him or otherwise been aware of his presence, but that kind of anecdotal evidence seems questionable and lacking in substance. If, on the other hand, God occasionally manifested himself in some physical way equivalent to the noise or turbulence I spoke of earlier, then we might have cause to look up and wonder. Of course, we would most likely look for a *natural* explanation for the manifestation before we concluded that this was a supernatural manifestation.

The Loch Ness monster, if such a thing does exist, might be a number of things, or it might be nothing at all. The most popular explanation for what people imagine they are seeing is the Plesiosaur, which is not a dinosaur, but rather a prehistoric aquatic reptile which lived in the warm seas which surrounded Scotland 70 million years ago. It is hardly likely that we would still be sighting something that lived so long ago. The other problem is that a monster probably has no interest in being sighted or displaying itself, it just goes about swimming in the depths of the lake and, perhaps, occasionally coming up for a touch of air, if it's the kind of creature that needs to do that.

God on the other hand, if he does exist, might be thought of in the same way as the monster. If he does exist, the most likely candidate is what most people who believe in him imagine him to be—some supreme, personal being who created us, cares for us and wants us to know him and believe in him. Like the Plesiosaur, that seems very unlikely given the lack of evidence. The being imagined could be any number of things and not necessarily the God of traditional religious belief. He could be a very advanced super-intelligence, an alien, an entity who for us, would be indistinguishable from a god. He or she or it, might not be personal at all, but rather some kind of cosmic force.

Carl Sagan's 1985 science-fiction novel, *Contact*, has the scientist Ellie, transported by a dodecahedron through a series of wormholes to a place near the center of our Milky Way Galaxy. She finds herself many light-years from Earth on an Earth-like beach where she encounters an extraterrestrial who has taken on the form of her dead father, so as to put her at ease in her strange environment. He tells her that he is part of a race of aliens with a project to alter the properties of the universe, and that unimaginably advanced as they are in relation to humans, the wormholes were built by still more advanced beings who have left their messages in the language of mathematics. It is far more likely that sometime in the future we will encounter beings like these before we will encounter God.

If, however, we are to assume that the mysterious presence or being religion speaks of *is* the traditional God, then, unlike the prehistoric aquatic reptile in Loch Ness, he *would* want to be seen or heard. Why? Because believing in him, obeying him is supposed to be essential for our salvation, our only way of entering an eternal hereafter. Deliberately refusing to believe in him might well result in our spending an eternity suffering in hell. Given the enormity of the consequences involved in such a belief or non-belief, it would seem absolutely essential that such a being should make his existence clear and unambiguous. As it is God, the much-reported being, is renowned for his hiddenness and silence and the few chosen individuals who claim to have sighted him, give disparate and varied accounts of their sightings. We have only their word for it.

This is why most of the time, most of the people around us live their lives, enjoy their families, relationships, jobs and fun times, as well as the scenery and give little if any thought to God's existence. It is not that they are ignoring him—what is there to ignore?—it is that *he seems to be ignoring them*. Just as it would be irrational for us to become obsessed with the existence of something like the Loch Ness monster for which there is no real evidence, so it would be equally irrational for us to spend time focused on the existence of God, for whom there is no real evidence. When I ceased to be a believer, I felt much less anxious about the people around me who don't practice any kind of religious faith but who seem to be decent and good in every other way.

Some liberal apologists for Christianity try to draw a distinction between God and the institutional religion. God remains sacrosanct, but religion is a work of the human imagination. But by separating religion from

God and refusing to concede that God *too* might be a work of the human imagination, what we are left with is a God who really cannot communicate with us. He has no instrument of communication, no sacred text, no prophets, no son. If these are all our ways of imagining the unimaginable God, why not treat God as the Buddha did? If the ways of God are so inscrutable as to defy further enquiry, then as Buddha said, even if God exists, what practical difference does it make to one's life here and now? Buddha taught that the God-idea has its origin in anxiety and fear and may be considered one of our human cravings for comfort or immortality. He said that there did not seem to be very much evidence to support the idea of a Creator-God; that the belief itself, was simply not necessary. Buddhists like millions of atheists and free-thinkers live useful, happy, meaningful lives without belief in a god.

If there is some kind of mind or power behind all of reality, it is too transcendent for we mere humans to detect it, so why be concerned about its existence? If it means us to know who or what it is, it will have to make contact with us. All the historic claims for such contact remain unconvincing. Christians of course, will object that God *has* made contact and that we know that God exists and what he is like because we know Jesus. I no longer find this a convincing argument at all. It is not convincing to anyone but Christians. It is not convincing to Jews. It is arguable that Jesus is no more a revelation of God than was Krishna, and I certainly find the character and teachings of Buddha to be more inspiring than those of Jesus, and Buddha didn't believe in God. The point is that it is the existence of God that must first be established before we can start talking about the possibility that that God became incarnate in a particular human being.

As far as religion is concerned I am no longer under the illusion that it has anything further to teach me about reality. I agree absolutely with that recurring theme in most of Richard Holloway's works, and that theme, that idea, is the only real 'revelation' that I now subscribe to.

My working assumption is that the discoveries we have made in our quest for meaning have all come from us, are all human constructs. Their existence is testimony to our extraordinary creativity as a species. We are constantly digging for meaning, searching for understanding ...

All the ladders start in the human heart: We generate the material; we create the images; the art comes through us or, to be more precise, through people of genius, inspired individuals. ... . If we stop trying to establish the independent existence of a supernatural reality that overwhelms us from the outside, we are left with the profound fact of the depth and richness of our own unconscious from which insights and challenges emerge into our minds. The revelations of our religious imagination are among the most powerful of our creations ... . all the ladders start in our own heart.[1]

Summing Up

I like the scientific spirit—the holding off, the being sure but not too sure,
The willingness to surrender ideas when the evidence is against them:
This is ultimately fine—it always keeps the way beyond open –
always gives life, thought, affection, the whole man,
a chance to try over again after a mistake—after a wrong guess.
                            –Walt Whitman, Camden Conversations
Re-examine all you have been told. Dismiss what insults your soul.
                            –Walt Whitman

Atheists who were once religious believers are people who have simply followed through on all the implications of their religion's constant revision and reinterpretation of its dogmas and practices. Religious believers who hesitate to follow through on such implications, remain believers, but always of a more qualified sort. A modern religion like Mormonism illustrates this principle very clearly. In less than 200 years, Mormonism has gone through major shifts in its doctrines and practices, all of which have been well documented.

In its first century alone, it revised its doctrine of God, no minor point, several times. It also abandoned certain practices, most notably, the doctrine of plural marriage (1890). In its second century (1930 to the present), it has revised its 'sacred' Temple Endowment ritual several times and abandoned its teaching of God's 'curse' on the 'Negro' which previously banned Blacks from being ordained in the Church (1978). In recent decades, as the Church has come under even greater scrutiny, it has qualified or revised its doctrine of God—again!—and edited or deleted aspects of its story of salvation. In every instance, the changes do not *add* to what has already been 'revealed', but rather *delete* teachings or practices that have become difficult to maintain or defend. The God who spoke so openly and frequently through the founder, Joseph Smith, now has very little if anything to say and seems to want to change what he has already said. As I said before, in the case of the Temple Endowment, a badly-kept secret ceremony, the content deleted has been content that Mormons themselves found disturbing or unacceptable.

The language of accommodation employed to explain all of these changes, is the very language which provokes doubt and questioning about the inspired leadership of the Church and the nature of revelation itself. Any study of the many ex-Mormon websites will indicate that it is the changes, editing, cover-ups, revisions and omissions that continue to be a primary cause of the thousands of annual defections from the Church. Simon G. Southerton is a senior research scientist with the Commonwealth Scientific and Industrial research Organization (CSIRO) in Canberra, Australia. His research is in the Department of Biochemistry, specialising in molecular biology.

During active membership of the Church for nearly thirty years, he served as a missionary elder, later married in the Temple and served for two years as a bishop (leader of a local church or 'ward'). Southerton is the author of *Losing a Lost Tribe: Native Americans, DNA and the Mormon Church* (2004). His book reflects the latest DNA research which effectively demolishes the claim of the Book of Mormon that native Americans and Polynesians are descended from ancient seafaring Israelites. The implication of that is unambiguous. The Book of Mormon is *not* a historical record, is *not* inspired scripture and was probably produced by a man who was *not* a prophet! That leaves the 'keystone of our religion' well and truly shattered.

Since we live in the same city, I met with Simon on a number of occasions and we discussed our mutual disillusionment with Mormonism. Simon resigned as a bishop and was later excommunicated, as I was some years earlier. Like a lot of ex-Mormons who do not find any faith-community to replace Mormonism, Simon is now quite content to call himself an atheist. Something about having had an intimate experience with the falsehood of their religion, provides people with an insight into the questionable nature of *all* religions. As Cota remarked in Cicero's *On the Nature of the Gods,* he was quite happy to take his religion on trust from tradition, 'but the more it is defended by argument, the more doubtful it becomes.' It was never Southerton's intention to 'offend or to offer advice in matters of faith, for these are issues which each person has to decide on his or her own'. Nevertheless the whole point of writing his book was to point out that 'for fellow Mormons who believe American Indians and Polynesians are largely descended from ancient Israelites, the recent findings of science may compel them, as I was compelled, to re-evaluate their thinking.'[1]

In the conclusion to his book, he expresses his disappointment that too many Mormons allow their feelings to cover over the facts and that the Mormon Church itself allows its scholarly researchers and apologists to 'subject the Book of Mormon to radical reinterpretation to accommodate their findings'. He understands the obstacles facing the Church and observes that:

> The real stumbling block is not the failure to find evidence for horses, metallurgy, or the wheel in the New World, or the fact that there is no evidence for a Hebrew influence in Mesoamerica, or the preponderance of Asian DNA among living Native Americans and Polynesians. The real challenge comes from a failure to openly confront the evidence and state what it means for the church, as well as a failure to accommodate the apologists, who themselves feel hemmed in by the church's insistence that members believe tenets that are clearly untrue.[2]

For decades, Christian writers, myself included at one stage in my life, have written books attacking the Mormon faith and questioning its claims. Evangelicals in particular, maintain a whole industry of apologetics devoted to explaining why *other* people's beliefs are not true. They are in fact, so enthusiastic in this endeavour, that they write books critical of Roman Catholicism, calling *it* a 'false gospel.' The irony of this is that before the Sixteenth century, the vast majority of Christians were Roman Catholics and had been so for a thousand years.

The Protestant Reformation itself, represents a massive, and one might say, a radical re-interpretation of traditional Christianity. The radical re-interpretation has since spawned innumerable radical re-interpretations of its own, all justifying their separateness on the basis of what the Bible *really* teaches. While relations between Catholics and Protestants have vastly improved, stories of 'conversion' working both ways still attract interest. Whether it is Thomas Howard, writing *Evangelical is Not Enough* in 1984, and eventually converting to Roman Catholicism—see his *On Being Catholic*, 1997, or George Barna, founder of The Barna Group (which markets research specializing in studying the religious beliefs and behavior of Americans), who gave up Catholicism to become an Evangelical Christian, the traffic continues to be a two-way street.

Mark A. Knoll is the McManis Professor of Christian Thought at evangelical Wheaton College, Illinois and author of many books. In 2005 he wrote *Is the Reformation Over? An Evangelical Assessment of Contemporary Roman Catholicism,* in conjunction with Carolyn Nystrom. While he is optimistic that God is working to bring Catholics and Protestants closer together, he has no doubt that fundamental differences remain.

> The divide is deep because it is a question of different (and deeply ingrained) practice as much as or *more* than it is a question of conflicting doctrines. In the best book ever published by an American Catholic on evangelical Christianity, William Shea phrases the essential issue like this: 'Are we to imagine that salvation is a gift to individuals

who then go on to decide to form a church, or does God's grace constitute a community of lost souls (say, Twelve of them!) by membership in which the souls are no longer lost? This is the heart of the issue: is it an entire people or individual persons God saved? [3]

Significantly the question of how salvation is to be understood continues to stand at the core of much of the differences and divisions *within* Christianity. Evangelicals exposing the theological shortcomings and heresies of groups and movements outside the mainstream, are not quite so forthcoming at focusing on divisions within the mainstream. The point is, that all religions exhibit internal weaknesses and contradictions as a result of their being human creations rather than responses to divine revelation, and each is confident that it alone has a fuller apprehension of the truth. Each has to work hard at staying abreast of the latest scientific discoveries in both the natural world and in the world of human nature. At the same time, with the passage of time, each has to deal with the growing lack of substantive evidence for its foundation claims.

A number of times in this book I have described Judaism as the initial and on-going critique of Christian claims for salvation. Judaism today may be a minnow compared with the great leviathan of Christianity, but as the original custodian of the Bible, it will always be in a strong position to point out the falsity of Christian claims to have superseded it. Mormonism is a nineteenth-century American movement within Christianity, in the same sense that Christianity was a first century Jewish movement within Judaism. In both cases, the parent-religion was critical of the nature of its offspring. As Fawn Brodie remarked, Mormonism 'was no mere dissenting sect. It was a real religious creation, one intended to be to Christianity as Christianity was to Judaism: that is, a reform and a consummation.'[4]

Each new religious movement—the prophets of Israel, Jesus and his apostles, Muhammad, the Buddha—claims to be in possession of further light, new knowledge, 'final' disclosures from God. Rather than clearly instructing his messengers what to say, so as to avoid confusion and division, God appears to allow his messengers to imagine whatever *they* want to say. If he ever truly spoke to Abraham and Moses, then there would have been no need of Christ and the cross. And if he had ever truly spoken to or through Christ 'in these last days by a Son whom he appointed heir of all things' (Hebrews 1:2), then there would have been no need for the prophet Muhammad, much less for Joseph Smith, centuries after him. But then, if the Buddha had truly achieved enlightenment without any help from God, five hundred years before Christ, Judaism, Christianity and Islam, not to mention Mormonism, might well have been stillborn.

So long as Christianity remains connected to the Bible, or at least that major part of it which is Hebrew or Jewish, it will always stand, however impressively, on shaky ground. The foundation, the proclamation of the cross or atoning sacrifice of Christ is, despite all the historic and laboured explanations mounted in its defence, incoherent, unbelievable and indefensible. If it should remain a doctrine considered worthy of belief, then it will, as it always has, be one that reflects very badly on the nature of God.

'World-conquering fiction', 'absurd and immoral', 'immature mythology', these are the judgments of Judaism on Christianity. Could a humanist say it any better? Perhaps the ultimate argument against the atoning death of Christ is not any argument we can present today, but rather its rejection by the Jews. Of course Christian apologists will always argue as the apostle Paul did, that the Jews have been blinded by Satan, hence his 'great sorrow and anguish of heart' (Romans 9:2) and desire and prayer that they might be saved (10:1). Israel 'failed to obtain what it was seeking' (Romans 11:7). But the more obvious explanation for their refusal to accept the Gospel, is that it simply made no sense.

Columnist David Klinghoffer writes: 'In advocating these (doctrines like the Trinity and the Incarnation), Christians asked Jews to embrace beliefs that both contradicted logic and denied certain basic principles about God. Contradictions of that kind, the Jews said, they could not accept.'⁵ This same Jewish author believes that the Jewish rejection of Jesus points to an essential insecurity at the heart of Christian theology, namely the failure of Jesus and his immediate followers to make the case to Jesus' own people. I would suggest that even Christians today are suspecting that their theologians and ministers are failing to make the case.

It is not difficult to find tomes of Christian theology struggling with these contradictions and challenges to logic. Until I was 'deconverted', it was almost shameful to admit that you were looking for a rational or logical explanation for any doctrine, because that showed a lack of faith and trust in God. My struggle to maintain, and because of my position as a minister, to explain the Faith, left me unsatisfied that it could ultimately be defended. Judaism continues to say what it has been saying for 2,000 years.

> Still granting the infiniteness of the sin of the first man and woman, and even granting that it's meaningful to speak of God as having a 'Son', there was *no need* to atone for the great sin by God's offering up the incarnate and second person of the Trinity. God can forgive any crime, finite or infinite, if He wishes, but Christians made it sound as if He were bound by some law beyond Himself, as if he could not forgive mankind without letting his Son die on the cross. Of course there is no law beyond God.⁶

If we are going to allow the Bible to speak in its own terms, then it is the *Jewish* rather than the Christian interpretation that must prevail. Once it does then the fiction of the Cross of Christ collapses and sadly, as Paul mooted, 'if justification comes through the Law, then Christ died for nothing' (Galatians 2:21). As a Jew, Paul may have suspected that the Jesus he never actually knew personally, had indeed 'died for nothing' or died in vain, but compelled by his own bewildering and creative take on Judaism, he fashioned the theological apparatus that transformed Jesus of Nazareth into the Saviour-Christ. He may even have been aware that Jesus came to see himself as the 'Son of Man' who would suffer for the sake of Israel, but that suffering was supposed to be a prelude to the coming of God's Kingdom, not an act of redemption for the forgiveness of sins.

The Jews of Jesus' day were certainly looking for a Messiah who would deliver the people from oppression and rule the world as the Lord's anointed King. According to the early evangelists of the gospel, Jesus was that figure. Shortly after the report of the resurrection in Luke's Gospel, a disciple called Cleopas on the road to Emmaus, says clearly who he thought Jesus was. 'Jesus of Nazareth was a prophet mighty in deed and word before God and all the people' (Luke 24:19). The apostle Peter, likewise addressing crowds in Jerusalem, declared, 'Jesus of Nazareth, a man attested to you by God with deeds of power, wonders and signs that God did through him among you as you yourselves know—this man handed over to you according to the definite plan and foreknowledge of God, you crucified and killed ... But God raised him up'(Acts 2:22,23).

It would be left to the creeds of the Fourth century to make more of this man than the apostles did, indeed to make him one and the same with God. But in the gospels Jesus is always regarded as subordinate to the Father. The Father empowered him, the Father decreed that he should suffer and die, and the Father, if the apostles are to be believed, raised him from the dead. This *man*—they could have said 'God incarnate', but didn't—was somehow, unexpectedly, despite his death, the Messiah Israel awaited.

The disciples continued to believe that Jesus would return soon and vindicate their faith in him as he established the kingdom and rule of God on earth. Without that expectation, his death really had no meaning and he *would* have died in vain. With that expectation they could live, for the moment, in hope. But the hope was never realised. 'What happened as that expectation of redemption was delayed and as more Gentiles joined this community is the story of the Church, of Christianity.'[7] That story, essentially Paul's story, is the 'world-conquering fiction' that continues to this day. It is a story which is inherently flawed and difficult to explain, as centuries of Christian theology have demonstrated. But it is a story that will continue to be told for as long as that first century hope remains unrealised.

It may well be, that just as Christian scholars are re-discovering the 'Jewishness of Jesus' and listening more to what Jewish writers have to say about Christianity, that they will also continue to acknowledge the original Jewishness of Christianity and question whether or not a new religion was necessary at all. That is probably a forlorn hope, but all religions evolve and change as reason continues to challenge faith. That challenge is now centuries old and the fact that nonbelievers in the world now number more than a billion and are growing in substantial numbers every year, is testimony to the power of human curiosity and questioning and the pursuit of truth divorced from religious claims.

Philosopher Kai Nielsen's question to an agnostic is relevant to our discussion about the credibility of the Christian dogma of salvation. It reminds me of the choices I faced over a number of years and of the struggle involved in coming to a settled conviction about the matter. As my Christian friends often remind me, 'everyone has doubts', as if to suggest that such doubts might only be a test of faith rather than a clue that faith is unwarranted. For some Christians, the doubts and questions *are* regarded as 'tests' of their loyalty or faithfulness to God. There is nothing sinful about doubting, they reassure you, provided you don't take your doubts too seriously. They put their doubts aside and shelve the troubling questions. After all, what does the old proverb from the 'Old' Testament book of Ecclesiastes 12:12 say? 'Of anything beyond these, my child, beware. Of making many books there is no end, and much study is a weariness of the flesh.' In most instances, the believer will consider *any* study which might address her doubts to be *too much* study. Nielsen challenges us to think.

> The thing to ask is whether the doubts leading to a suspension of judgment are actually sufficient to *justify* such a suspension or, everything

considered, (1) would a leap of faith be more justified or (2) would the overcoming of doubt in the direction of atheism be more reasonable? Or is it the case that there is no way of making a rational decision here or of reasonably deciding what one ought to do or believe?[8]

In this case, faced with the claim of Christian salvation and all it implies about the nature of humankind, the nature of God, the danger of being eternally lost, and the inability of God to forgive without punishment or a human sacrifice, wouldn't the overcoming of doubt about these strange and incomprehensible concepts, be achieved by moving in the direction of atheism? The consequences of irrational thought are that we remain imprisoned in wilful ignorance and committed to a God who is a chimera, a fiction, Dorothy's 'Great and terrible Humbug' in the Kingdom of Oz, the invisible, silent, inert one, a deity who is a reflection of all our own thoughts and imaginings.

Notes

Introduction

1. Robert G. Ingersoll, *www.theingersolltimes.com* quote. See also his essay, *The Creeds*.
2. Alister McGrath, *Studies in Doctrine,* Zondervan, Grand Rapids, 1997, pp. 453, 460
3. Lewis A. Hart, *A Jewish Reply to Christian Evangelists,* Bloch Publishing Company, New York, 1906. Historical Reproduction by BilioLife, LLC, p. 3.

Chapter 1. The 'Good News'?

1. Franz Rosenzweig, *Judaism Despite Christianity: The 1916 wartime correspondence between Eugen Rosenstock-Huessy & Franz Rosenzweig* (Edited by Eugen Rosenstock-Huessy, The University of Chicago Press, Chicago and London, 1935/2011, p. 112.

Chapter 2. Two Testaments, Two Bibles

1. Jacob Neusner, *Jews and Christians: The Myth of a Common Tradition,* SCM Press, London and trinity press International, Philadelphia, p. 28.
2. Rev. Dr. A. Lukyn Williams, *The Doctrines of Modern Judaism Considered,* SPCK, London, First Edition, 1939, p. 159.
3. C.S. Lewis, Introduction to *St. Athanasius on the Incarnation,* translated from the Greek by Sister Penelope Lawson, CSMV, A.R. Mowbray & Co. London, 1975, p.4.
4. Eugene B. Borowitz, *Liberal Judaism,* Union of American Hebrew Congregations, New York, 1984, p. 80.

Chapter 3. The Fall and Human Lostness

1. I. Howard Marshall, *Aspects of The Atonement: Cross and Resurrection in the Reconciling of God and Humanity,* Paternoster, London, Colorado Springs, Hyderabad, 2007, p. 3.
2. Human Origins Program; www.humanorigins.si.edu
3. Denis Alexander, *Creation or Evolution? Do We have to Choose?* Monarch Books, 2008, p. 351.
4. John S. Dickerson, *The Great Evangelical Recession,* Baker Books, Grand Rapids, 2013, p.26.
5. Denis Alexander, *Creation or Evolution: Do we have to Choose?* Monarch Books, Oxford and Grand Rapids, 2008, pp. 242-3.
6. Ibid., 243.
7. Barbara Tuchman, *The March of Folly,* Abacus, London, 1985, p. 434.
8. Russell Blackford, Interview in the *Philotoric,* July 14, 2014. https://thephilotoric.wordpress.com
9. Norman L. Geisler and Frank Turek, *I Don't Have Enough Faith to Be an Atheist* Crossway Books, Wheaton Illinois, 2004, p. 390.
10. Hans Kung, *Credo: The Apostles' Creed Explained for Today,* Wipf and Stock Publishers, Eugene Oregon, 1992, pp. 21,22.
11. Robert G. Ingersoll, *The Creeds.* Article at www.theingersolltimes.com

Chapter 4. Down the Rabbit Hole—Part 1

1. Robert D. Brinsmead, *The Chamber of Horrors,* essay found on Brinsmead's website: www.bobbrinsmead.com essay, p. 10.
2. Ibid., p. 11
3. Robert D. Brinsmead, *New Year Essay, Part Two,* 2001, p. 15.
4. Hans Kung, *On Being a Christian,* Translated by Edward Quinn, Collins, Fount Paperbacks, Glasgow, 1974, p. 424.
5. Ibid., p. 424
6. Ibid., p. 426
7. *Catechism of the Catholic Church,* Second Edition, St. Paul's Publications, Sydney, Article 3:1330, pp. 335-336.
8. Ibid. 1366-67

9. *On Being a Christian,* Translated by Edward Quinn, Collins, Fount Paperbacks, Glasgow, 1974, p. 435.
10. John Stott, *The Cross of Christ,* 20th Anniversary Edition, Inter-Varsity Press, Nottingham, 1986,2006, p. 190.
11. Ibid., p. 191
12. Ibid., pp. 398-99
13. Max Brod, *Paganism, Christianity, Judaism,* The University of Alabama Press, 1970, p.172.
14. *The Cross of Christ,* op. cit., p. 158.
15. Ibid., p. 163.
16. A.L. De Silva, *Beyond Belief: A Buddhist Critique of Fundamentalist Christianity,* Three Gem Publications, Sydney, 1994, p. 35.
17. Rabbi Shmuley Boteach, *Kosher Jesus,* Gefen Publishing House, Jerusalem, 2012, pp. 169-70.
18. *The Cross of Christ,* op. cit., pp. 166, 187.
19. Jurgen Moltmann, *The Crucified God,* SCM Press, London, 1974. p. 243.
20. Ibid., p. 244
21. Gunapala Dharmasiri, *A Buddhist Critique of the Christian Concept of God,* Lake House Investments, Colombo, 1974, pp.228-229.
22. Ibid., p. 230
23. *The Cross of Christ,* op. cit., p. 173.
24. Ibid., p. 179
25. Ibid., p. 180

Chapter 5. Down the Rabbit Hole—Part 2

1. Website of the Archdiocese of Sydney Anglicans. Question & Answer section, Anglican Media Centre, 2014. www.anglicanmedia.com.au
2. Robert Shaw, *The Reformed Faith: An Exposition of The Westminster Confession of Faith,* Christian Focus Publications, Inverness, 1974, Reprint. Chapter 3, 'Concerning God's Eternal Decrees'.
3. Mark Oppenheimer, *Evangelicals find themselves in the Midst of a Calvinist Revival,* report in *The New York Times,* January 3, 2014.

4. Collin Hanson, *Young, Restless, Reformed: A Journalist's Journey with the New Calvinists,* Crossway Books, Wheaton, Illinois, 2008, p. 67.
5. Al Mohler, a 2000 television interview on *Larry King Live,* http://en.wikipedia.org/wiki/Albert_Mohler
6. Denton Lotz, Comment by the General Secretary of the Baptist World Alliance, (BWA), *Christianity Today* report, June 1, 2004. www.christianitytoday.com
7. Rabbi Stuart Federow, author of *Judaism and Christianity: A Contrast,* iUniverse, Inc. Bloomington, 2012, p. 200.
8. Tom Wright, *Justification: God's Plan and God's Vision,* SPCK, London, 2009, pp. 221-2
9. Blurb from back cover of Ian Howard Marshall's *Aspects of the Atonement,* Paternoster, London, Colorado Springs, Hyderabad, 2007.
10. Ibid., *Aspects of the Atonement,* pp. 5-6.
11. John Stott and David L. Edwards, *Essentials: A liberal-evangelical dialogue,* Hodder & Stoughton, London, Sydney, 1988, p. 318.
12. Scott McKnight, *The Day Evangelicalism Shook over Hell,* www.patheos.com/blogs/…/07…the-day-evangelicalism-shook-on-hell July 7, 2014.
13. Wayne Grudem, *Systematic Theology,* Inter-Varsity Press, Nottingham, 2007, p. 823.
14. *Aspects of the Atonement,* op. cit., p. 11.
15. Ibid., p. 12
16. Ibid., p. 30
17. Ibid., p. 36
18. Ibid., pp. 44-45
19. Ibid., p. 56
20. Ibid., p. 57
21. Ibid., p. 62
22. Ibid., p. 95
23. Ibid., p. 136
24. E.P. Sanders, *Paul and Palestinian Judaism,* SCM Press, London, 1977/1993, p. 499.
25. Ibid., p. 443

26. Ibid. p. 443
27. Hyam Maccoby, *The Myth-Maker: Paul and the Invention of Christianity*, HarperSan Francisco, Harper Collins Publishers, new York, 1987.

Chapter 6. Engaging with a Liberal Theologian (John Hick)

1. The Official John Hick website.
2. John Hick, *The Metaphor of God Incarnate: Christology in a Pluralistic Age*, Second edition, Westminster, John Knox Press, Louisville and London, 2005, p. 113.
3. Ibid., p. 116
4. Ibid., p. 116
5. Ibid., p. 117
6. Ibid., p. 119
7. Ibid., p. 122
8. Ibid., p. 122
9. Ibid., p. 122
10. Rabbis Dennis Prager and Joseph Telushkin *The Nine Questions People Ask About Judaism,* A Touchstone Book, Simon & Schuster, New York, 1975, 1986, p. 85.
11. Dennis Prager, *When Forgiveness is a Sin,* article in *Reader's Digest* magazine, May 1998.
12. *The Nine Questions People Ask about Judaism,* op. cit., p. 82.
13. *The Metaphor of God Incarnate,* op. cit., p. 123.
14. E. P. Sanders, *Jesus and Judaism,* Fortress Press, Minneapolis, 1985, p. 332.
15. *The Metaphor of God Incarnate,* op. cit., pp. 124-125.
16. Ibid., pp. 176, 181.
17. John Hick lecture, *Believable Christianity,* Annual October series on Radical Christian Faith at Carrs Lane URC Church, Birmingham, October 5, 2006. From John Hick: The Official Website. www.johnhick.org.ik/article16.html

Chapter 7. The Twilight of Atheism?

1. Alister McGrath, *The Twilight of Atheism: The Rise and Fall of Disbelief in the Modern World.* Rider, London, Sydney, 2004, pp. 126-127.

2. Ibid., p. 275
3. Ibid., p. 275
4. Ibid., pp. 193-195
5. Ibid., p. 215
6. Alister McGrath, *Studies in Doctrine: Understanding Doctrine, The Trinity, Jesus and Justification by Faith,* Zondervan, Grand Rapids, 1997, p. 453.
7. Ibid., p. 453
8. Ibid., p. 453.
9. *Catechism of the Catholic Church*, Second Edition, St. Paul's Publications, Sydney, Chapter 3, Article 1: Section III, No. 153, p.41 Article 3:1330.
10. Ibid., pp. 404, 467
11. Ibid., p. 455.
12. Ibid., P. 455.
13. Ibid., p. 460

Chapter 8. Who Speaks for God?

1. Richard Carrier, *Why I am Not a Christian.* infidels.org/library/modern/richard_carrier/whynotchristian.html
2. *Hymns of the Church of Jesus Christ of Latter-day Saints,* 2nd Edition, Published by The Church of Jesus Christ of Latter-day Saints, Salt Lake City, 1985, Hymn 19.
3. Pope Pius XII Encyclical *Munificentissimus Deus,* November 1, 1950; and Pope Pius IX, Doctrine of the Immaculate Conception, Apostolic Constitution *Ineffabilis Deus*, December 8, 1854.
4. *Doctrine and Covenants*, Section 1, revelation given through Joseph Smith at Hiram, Ohio, November 1, 1831. Published by The Church of Jesus Christ of Latter-day Saints, Salt lake City, 1996.
5. Gerald and Sandra Tanner, *The Changing World of Mormonism,* Moody Press Chicago, 1980, p. 318.
6. James A. Lindsay, *God Doesn't; We Do: Only Humans Can Solve Human Challenges,* CreateSpace Independent Publishing Platform, 2012.
7. Mark P. Leone, *Roots of Modern Mormonism,* Harvard University Press, Cambridge Massachusetts, 1979, pp. 147, 171.

8. Fawn M. Brodie, *No Man Knows my History: The Life of Joseph Smith, the Mormon Prophet,* Second Edition, Revised and Enlarged, Alfred A. Knopf, New York, 1976, p. viii
9. C. S. Lewis, *The Great Divorce,* Collins, Fontana Books, Glasgow, 1974, p. 71.
10. John Hick, *The Rainbow of Faiths: Critical Dialogues on religious Pluralism.* Blurb on back cover of the First American Edition, Westminster, John Knox Press, Louisville, Kentucky, 1995.
11. John Hick, *The Rainbow of Faiths: Critical Dialogues on religious Pluralism*, SCM Press, London, 1995, p. 15.
12. Ibid., p. 16
13. Ibid., p. 19
14. Ibid., p. 47
15. Ibid., p. 50
16. Ibid., p. 60
17. John Hick, *The Metaphor of God Incarnate: Christology in a Pluralistic Age,* Second edition, Westminster, John Knox Press, Louisville and London, 2005, p. 182.
18. Jesse Bering, *The God Instinct: The Psychology of Souls, Destiny and the Meaning of Life*, Nicholas Brealey Publishing, London, 2010, p. 37.
19. *Metaphor of God Incarnate,* op. cit., p. 183.
20. Ibid., p. 184.

Chapter 9. Monster of Handbag?

1. John F. Haught, *God and the New Atheism: A Critical Response to Dawkins, Harris and Hitchens,* Westminster, John Knox Press, Louisville and London, 2008, p. 92.
2. Tom Frame, *Losing my Religion: Unbelief in Australia,* University of New South Wales Press, Sydney, 2009, p. 292.
3. Ibid., p. 293
4. Ibid., p. 297
5. Ibid., p. 294

6. Ibid., p. 295
7. Ibid., p. 299
8. Ibid., p. 300
9. Ibid., p. 301
10. Ibid., p. 302
11. Ibid., p. 303
12. Ibid., p. 303
13. Ibid., p. 304.
14. Mark Thompson, *What is the Gospel?* Article on the website of Sydney Anglicans, www.sydneyanglicans.net Also found at acl.asn.au/the-thirty-nine-articles, p. 5.
15. Ibid., p. 6
16. Ibid., p. 7
17. Ibid., p. 7
18. Ibid., p. 8
19. Ibid., p. 8
20. Ibid., pp. 89.
21. Ibid., p. 9.
22. Scott Cowdell, *Understanding Religious Decline,* article found in: www.anglicancg.org.au/articles/53/understanding-religious-decline. June 28, 2013, p. 1.
23. Ibid., p. 2-3
24. Ibid., p. 3
25. Ibid., p. 3
26. Os Guinness, *Unspeakable: Facing Up to the Challenge of Evil,* Harper, San Francisco, New York, 2006, p. 226.
27. Ibid., p. 238.
28. *Understanding Religious Decline,* op. cit., p. 3.
29. Ibid., p. 4
30. Ibid., p. 4
31. Ibid., p. 4

32. Ibid., p. 4.
33. Ibid., p. 4.

Chapter 10. The Man behind the Veil

1. *The Morning Breaks,* from Hymns of The Church of Jesus Christ of Latter-day Saints, Published by The Church of Jesus Christ of Latter-day Saints, Salt lake City, 1985 Edition, No. 1.
2. Joseph Fielding McConkie and Robert L. Millet, *Sustaining and Defending the Faith,* Bookcraft, Salt Lake City, 1985, p. 102.
3. L. Frank Baum, *The Wonderful Wizard of Oz,* Penguin Books, Melbourne, 2010, p. 110.
4. Ibid., p. 111
5. Alma P. Burton, *Discourses of the Prophet Joseph Smith,* Deseret Book Company, Salt Lake City, Third Edition, Revised and Enlarged, 1965, pp. 262-3.
6. Marcus Tullius Cicero, *De NaturaDeorum –'The Nature of the Gods',* Book III, Section XXXIX, from Gutenberg's *Cicero's Tusculan Disputations,* by Marcus Tullius Cicero, p. 354. eBook or online at www.gutenberg.net
7. Malcolm Jeeves, *Neuroscience Psychology and Religion: Illusions, Delusions and Realities about Human Nature,* Templeton Foundation Press, West Conshohocken, Penn., 2009, p. 136.
8. Kevin Nelson, *The God Impulse: Is religion Hardwired into our Brains,* Simon & Schuster, London and New York, 2011, p. 258.
9. John S. Dickerson, *The Great Evangelical Recession: 6 Factors that Will Crash the American Church. . . and How to Prepare,* Baker Books, Grand Rapids, 2013, p. 22.
10. Ibid., p. 24
11. ibid., p. 24.
12. Ibid., p. 28
13. Barclay, *Fishers of Men,* Epworth Press, London, 1966, pp. 135-36.

Chapter 11. 'God is plain to them'?

1. Richard Holloway, *Doubts and Loves: What is Left of Christianity?* Canongate Books, Edinburgh, 2001, pp. 16, 40, 44.

Chapter 12. Summing Up

1. Simon Southerton, *Losing a Lost Tribe: Native Americans, DNA and the Mormon Church,* Signature Books, Salt Lake City, 2004, p. viii.

2. Ibid., p. 206.

3. Mark A. Knoll and Carolyn Nystrom, *Is the Reformation Over? An Evangelical Assessment of Contemporary Roman Catholicism,* Baker Academic, Grand Rapids & Paternoster, 2005, p 238-39.

4. Fawn M. Brodie, *No Man Knows My History: The Life of Joseph Smith, the Mormon Prophet,* Second Edition, Revised and Enlarged, Alfred A. Knopf, New York, 1976, p. viii.

5. David Klinghoffer, *Why the Jews rejected Jesus: The Turning Point in Western History.* Three Leaves Press, Doubleday, New York, 2005, p. 173.

6. Ibid., p. 176.

7. Daniel Boyarin, *The Jewish Gospels: The Story of the Jewish Christ,* The New Press, New York, 2012, p. 142.

8. Kai Nielsen, *Atheism and Philosophy,* Prometheus Books, Amherst, New York, 2005, p. 109.

BIBLIOGRAPHY

Alexander, Denis. *Creation or Evolution? Do We have to Choose?* Monarch Books, Oxford & Grand Rapids, 2008.

Anglican Media Centre. Website of the Archdiocese of Sydney Anglicans. Question & Answer section, www.anglicanmedia.com.au 2014.

Barclay, William. *Fishers of Men.* Epworth Press, London, 1966.

Baum, Frank L. *The Wonderful Wizard of Oz.* Penguin Books, Melbourne, 2010.

Bering, Jesse. *The God Instinct*: *The Psychology of Souls, Destiny and the Meaning of Life.* Nicholas Brealey Publishing, London, 2010,

Blackford, Russell. Interview in the *Philotoric,* July 14, 2014 https://thephilotoric.wordpress.com

Borowitz, Eugene B. *Liberal Judaism.* Union of American Hebrew Congregations, New York, 1984.

Boyarin, Daniel. *The Jewish Gospels: The Story of the Jewish Christ,* The New Press, New York, 2012

Brinsmead, Robert D. essay, *The Chamber of Horrors,* www.bobbrinsmead.com essay

Brodie, Fawn M. *No Man Knows my History: The Life of Joseph Smith the Mormon Prophet.* Second Edition, revised and Enlarged, Alfred A. Knopf, New York, 1976.

Burton, Alma P. *Discourses of the Prophet Joseph Smith.* Deseret Book Company, Salt Lake City, Third Edition, Revised and Enlarged, 1965.

Catechism of the Catholic Church, Second Edition, St. Paul's Publications, Sydney, 2004.

Carrier, Richard. *Why I am Not a Christian.* infidels.org/library/modern/richard_carrier/whynotchristian.html .

Church of Jesus Christ of Latter-day Saints, publisher of the *Doctrine and Covenants.* Salt Lake City, 1996.

Cicero, *On Living and Dying Well.* Translated with an Introduction and notes by Thomas Habinek, Penguin Books, London. 2012; Marcus Tullius Cicero, *De NaturaDeorum –'The Nature of the Gods',* Book III, Section XXXIX, from Gutenberg's *Cicero's Tusculan Disputations,* p . 354 eBook or online at www.gutenberg.net

Cowdell, Scott. *Understanding Religious Decline,* article found in: www.anglicancg.org.au/articles/53/understanding-religious-decline. June 28, 2013,

Dickerson, John S. *The Great Evangelical Recession: 6 Factors that Will Crash the American Church. . . and How to Prepare.* Baker Books, Grand Rapids, 2013.

De Silva, A.L. *Beyond Belief: A Buddhist Critique of Fundamentalist Christianity.* Three Gem Publications, Sydney, 1994.

Dharmasiri, Gunapala. *A Buddhist Critique of the Christian Concept of God.* Lake House Investments, Colombo, 1974.

Federow, Stuart. *Judaism and Christianity: A Contrast.* iUniverse, Inc. Bloomington, 2012.

Frame, Tom. *Losing my Religion: Unbelief in Australia.* University of New South Wales Press, Sydney, 2009.

Geisler, Norman L. and Turek, Frank. *I Don't Have Enough Faith to Be an Atheist.* Crossway Books, Wheaton Illinois, 2004 .

Grudem, Wayne. *Systematic Theology: An Introduction to Biblical Doctrine.* Inter-Varsity Press, Nottingham, 2007.

Guinness, Os. *Unspeakable: Facing Up to the Challenge of Evil.* Harper, San Francisco, New York, 2006.

Collin Hansen, *Young, Restless, Reformed: A Journalist's Journey with the New Calvinists.* Crossway Books, Wheaton Illinois, 2008.

Hart, Lewis A. *A Jewish Reply to Christian Evangelists,* Bloch Publishing Company, New York, 1906. Historical Reproduction by BiblioLife, LLC.

Haught, John F. *God and the New Atheism: A Critical Response to Dawkins, Harris and Hitchens.* Westminster. John Knox Press, Louisville and London, 2008

Heschel, Abraham Joshua. *A Passion for Truth.* A Jewish Lights Classic reprint, Jewish Lights Publishing, Woodstock, Vermont, 2004 (Fourth printing).

Hick, John. *The Metaphor of God Incarnate: Christology in a Pluralistic Age,* Second Edition. Westminster, John Knox Press, Louisville and London, 2005.

Hick, John. Lecture, *Believable Christianity,* Annual October series on Radical Christian Faith at Carrs Lane URC Church, Birmingham, www.johnhick.org.uk/article16.html October 5, 2006.

Hick, John. *The Rainbow of Faiths: Critical Dialogues on religious Pluralism.* SCM Press, London, 1995.

Hick, John. The Official John Hick website. www.johnhick.org.uk

Holloway, Richard. *Doubts and Loves: What is Left of Christianity?* Canongate Books, Edinburgh, 2001.

Human Origins Program; www.humanorigins.si.edu

Hymns of The Church of Jesus Christ of Latter-day Saints, Published by The Church of Jesus Christ of Latter-day Saints, Salt Lake City, 1985 Edition.

Ingersoll, Robert G. *The Creeds.* Article at www.theingersolltimes.com

Jeeves, Malcolm & Brown, Warren S. *Neuroscience Psychology and Religion: Illusions, Delusions and Realities about Human Nature.* Templeton Foundation Press, West Conshohocken, Penn., 2009.

Klinghoffer, David. *Why the Jews rejected Jesus: The Turning Point in Western History.* Three Leaves Press, Doubleday, New York, 2005.

Knoll, Mark A. and Nystrom, Carolyn, *Is the Reformation Over? An Evangelical Assessment of Contemporary Roman Catholicism,* Baker Academic, Grand Rapids & Paternoster, 2005.

Kung, Hans. *On Being a Christian.* Translated by Edward Quinn. Collins, Fount Paperbacks, 1974.

Kung, Hans. *Credo: The Apostles' Creed Explained for Today.* Wipf and Stock Publishers, Eugene, Oregon. 1992.

Leone, Mark P. *Roots of Modern Mormonism.* Harvard University Press, Cambridge, Massachusetts, 1979.

Lewis, C.S. Introduction to *St. Athanasius on the Incarnation*, translated from the Greek by Sister Penelope Lawson, CSMV. A.R. Mowbray & Co. London, 1975.

Lewis, C.S. *The Great Divorce.* Collins Fontana Books, Glasgow, 1974.

Lindsay, James A. *God Doesn't; We Do: Only Humans Can Solve Human Challenges.* CreateSpace Independent Publishing Platform, 2012.

Lotz, Denton. Comment by General Secretary of the Baptist World Alliance, (BWA), *Christianity Today* report, June 1, 2004. www.christianitytoday.com

Maccoby, Hyam. *The Myth-Maker: Paul and the Invention of Christianity.* HarperSan Francisco, Harper Collins Publishers, New York, 1987.

Marshall, I. Howard. *Aspects of The Atonement: Cross and Resurrection in the Reconciling of God and Humanity.* Paternoster, London, Colorado Springs, Hyderabad, 2007.

McConkie, Joseph Fielding and Millet, Robert L. *Sustaining and Defending the Faith.* Bookcraft, Salt Lake City, 1985.

McGrath, Alister. *The Twilight of Atheism: The Rise and Fall of Disbelief in the Modern World.* Rider. London, Sydney, 2004.

McGrath, Alister. *Studies in Doctrine: Understanding Doctrine, The Trinity, Jesus and Justification by Faith.* Zondervan, Grand Rapids, 1997.

McKnight, Scott. *The Day Evangelicalism Shook over Hell,* www.patheos.com/blogs/.../07...'the-day-evangelicalism-shook-on-hell July 7, 2014.

Mohler, Al. A 2000 television interview on *Larry King Live,* http://en.wikipedia.org/wiki/Albert_Mohler

Moltmann, Jurgen. *The Crucified God.* SCM Press, London, 1974.

Nelson, Kevin. *The God Impulse: Is religion Hardwired into our Brains?* Simon & Schuster, London, New York, 2011.

Neusner, Jacob. *Jews and Christians: The Myth of a Common Tradition.* SCM Press, London and Trinity Press International, Philadelphia, 1991.

Nielsen, Kai. *Atheism and Philosophy,* Prometheus Books, Amherst, New York, 2005.

Oppenheimer, Mark, *Evangelical find themselves in the Midst of a Calvinist Revival,* report in *The New York Times,* January 3, 2014.

Prager, Dennis and Telushkin, Joseph. *The Nine Questions People Ask About Judaism.* A Touchstone Book, Simon & Schuster, New York, 1975, 1986.

Prager, Dennis. *When Forgiveness is a Sin,* article in *Reader's Digest* magazine, May 1998.

Pope Pius XII Encyclical *Munificentissimus Deus,* November 1, 1950; and Pope Pius IX, Doctrine of the Immaculate Conception, Apostolic Constitution *Ineffabilis Deus,* December 8, 1854. w2.vatican.va/.../hf_p-xii_apc_19501101_munificentissimus-deus.html

Rosenstock-Huessy, Eugen. *Judaism Despite Christianity: The 1916 wartime correspondence between Eugen Rosenstock-Huessy and Franz Rosenzweig,* The University of Chicago Press, Chicago and London, 1935/2011.

Sanders, E. P. *Jesus and Judaism.* Fortress Press, Minneapolis, 1985.

Shaw, Robert. *The Reformed Faith: An Exposition of the Westminster Confession of Faith.* Christian Focus Publications, Inverness, 1974 reprint.

Southerton, Simon. *Losing a Lost Tribe: Native Americans, DNA and the Mormon Church,* Signature Books, Salt Lake City, 2004.

Stott, John. *The Cross of Christ.* 20th Anniversary Edition, Inter-Varsity Press, Nottingham, 1986, 2006.

Stott, John and Edwards, David L. *Essentials: A liberal-evangelical dialogue.* Hodder & Stoughton, London, Sydney, 1988.

Tanner, Gerald and Sandra. *The Changing World of Mormonism.* Moody Press, Chicago, 1980.

Thompson, Mark. *What is the Gospel?* Article on the website of Sydney Anglicans,

www.sydneyanglicans.net Also found at: acl.asn.au/the-thirty-nine-articles,

Tuchman, Barbara. *The March of Folly.* Abacus, London, 1985.

Wright, Tom. *Justification: God's Plan and God's Vision.* SPCK, London, 2009.

Williams, A. Lukyn. *The Doctrines of Modern Judaism Considered.* SPCK, London, First Edition, 1939.

INDEX

Achilles heel, viii, 11, 24, 38, 129
Adam and Eve, the Fall, 23-28, 44, 82, 140, 142
Alexander, Denis Dr., 27-29
All Souls, Langham Place, 43
Third Temple, 51
Anglican Doctrine of Election, 23, 43, 57-59, 67, 69, 91, 95, 133, 137, 138, 142, 146, 149
Angus, Samuel, 19
Atonement, blood, substitutionary, 1, 8, 10, 12, 14-17, 34-40, 43, 50, 52, 59-60, 67-70, 74-77, 80-89, 101, 130, 141, 166
Attenborough, David, 31
Australian Aborigines, 28
Baggini, Julian, 93
baptism of infants, 23
baptisms for dead, 153
Baptist World Alliance, 65
Barclay, William, 164
Baum, Frank L, 156

birth control, 113-114
Blackford, Russell, 29
Blacks and the priesthood, 113
Blocher, Henri, 68
Borowitz, Eugene, 17
Boteach, Shmuley Rabbi, 51
Bradlaugh, Charles, 92
Brinsmead, Robert D, 36
Brod, Max, 49
Brodie, Fawn, 181
Bruno, Giordano, 92
Buddha, 2, 127-128, 148, 175, 181-182
Buddhism, 21-22, 44, 50, 53-54
Calvin, John, 16, 59, 75
Calvinism, 59-60, 63-64, 167
Carrier, Richard, 103
Catechism of the Catholic Church, 41, 98
Catholicism, 64-65, 68, 98, 113, 160, 180
China, 127
Christadelphians, 150
Church College of Hawaii, 152
Cicero, 160, 179

cognitive dissonance, 29
Constantine, 127, 132
Contact, The Movie, 173
Copernicus, 81
Cosmos: A Spacetime Odyssey, 31
Cowdell, Scott, 131, 133, 142, 147
Cox, Brian, 31
Cranfield, E B, 49
Creation-Evolution, 166
Creationists, 25, 166
Cross of Christ, 3, 8, 32, 37, 43, 68, 71, 132, 183
Dalai Lama, 22
Darwinian Evolution, 26
David (King), 8, 13, 42, 45
Dawkins, Richard, 82
Dever, Mark, 63
Dharmasiri, Gunapala, 53
Dickerson, John, 27, 163
Dinosaurs, 171
Disney, Walt, 108
Doctrine and Covenants, 111-113
doubts, xi, 25, 29, 36, 78, 145, 162, 164-165, 185
Driscoll, Mark, 63
Edgecumbe Hughes, Philip, 69
Edwards, David L, 68
Endowment, Temple (Mormon), 113, 152, 153-155, 177-178
Epicureanism, 2, 92
Epicurus, 92
Epstein, Greg, 96, 146
Evangelicalism, 63, 69, 164
Evangelicals, 43, 65, 70, 79-81, 129, 162-164, 180-181
Federow, Rabbi Stuart, 66

Forgiveness, vii, 5-13, 15-19, 34, 38-39, 42, 47, 49, 54-55, 84-85, 87, 100-101, 155, 184
Forsyth, P T, 55, 70
Frame, Tom, 133, 135-137
Gandhi, Mahatma, 22, 44, 93
Geisler, Norman L, 30
Geneva, 59, 118
Ghana, 104
God's Eternal Decrees, 60
Goldstein, Rebecca, 91, 96
Gospel of John, 1, 107
grace, vii, 8, 11-12, 14-16, 23, 39, 42, 46, 53, 56, 58-62, 76, 98-99, 125
Graham, Billy, 63, 65, 77, 126
Grayling, Anthony, 93
Greenwich, 151
Grudem, Wayne, 69
Guinness, Os, 144
Han Dynasty, 127
handbag, 131, 144
Hansen, Collin, 64
Harris, Sam, 146, 161
Hart, Lewis A, ix
Haught, John F, x, 131
Hawaii Temple, 152
Hick, John, 77-79, 89-124
Hindu Brahmins, 54
Hinduism, 127, 148
Hitchens, Christopher, 82, 170
Holloway, Richard, 78, 103, 135, 175
Homo Erectus, Africa, 25
Homo Sapiens, 25-26, 82
Howard, Thomas, 180
Inerrancy, 65, 165
Ingersoll, Robert, viii, ix

Introduction to St. Athanasius, 11
On the Incarnation, 11
Islam, 64, 96, 121-123, 14 147, 182
Jainism, 92
Jeeves, Professor Malcolm, 161
Jefferson, Thomas, 92
Jesus, vii, ix, 1-22, 33, 37, 39, 40, 42-43, 45-48, 50-53, 55, 64, 66, 71-75, 85-89, 97, 100-101, 107-108, 119-121, 126-127, 131-132, 137-141, 144-145, 148, 150,155, 163, 166-167, 170, 175, 181, 183-184
Judaism, 4-11, 15, 18, 33-34, 36, 38, 41, 44, 46, 48, 50, 60, 72, 74-75, 83-84, 87, 100, 119, 120, 122, 132, 137, 182-183
Jurassic Park, 171
Ke Alaka'i , 158
Keller, Tim, 63
Kimball, Spencer W, 112
Kingdom of God, 87
Klinghoffer, David, 182
Knoll, Mark A, 180
Krishna, 127, 148, 175
Kung, Hans, 32, 39, 78, 98, 124, 169
Kurtz, Paul, xi, 93, 96
Leone, Mark P, 118
Lewis, C.S., 10-11, 123
liberal theology, 65, 79
Limited atonement, 16, 60
Lindsay, James A, 118
living prophets, 110-112
Loch Ness Monster, 172, 173-174
Lost in Space, 138
Lotz, Denton, 65
Luther, Martin, 35, 59

Maccoby, Hyam, 76
Maisel, Eric, 146
Maitreya, 148
Marshall, I Howard, 20, 35, 70
Mass, Eucharist, 16-17, 41
McConkie, Bruce R, 114
McConkie, Joseph Fielding, 153
McGrath, Alister, xi, 91-101
McKay, David, 110
McKnight, Scott, 69
Meslier, Father Jean, 82
Messiah, 19, 33, 75, 120, 184
Millet, Robert L, 153
Missionary elders (Mormon), 150
Mohler, Richard Albert, 64
Moltmann, Jurgen, 52-53
Monson, Thomas, 110
Morling College, 124
Mormonism, 75-76, 109-110, 116-123, 151-152, 155-160, 167, 177, 179, 181-182
Mormonism, Book of Mormon, 75, 111-112, 120-121, 150, 159-160, 167, 178-179
Muhammad, 111-112 121-123, 181-182
Native Americans, DNA, 178-179
Neanderthals, 25-26, 161
Nehru, Jawaharlal, 93
Nelson, Kevin, 161
Neusner, Jacob, 7-8
New Testament, 1, 4, 8, 13, 19-22, 32, 33, 39-40, 47, 49, 53, 55, 67-68, 72-76, 81-87, 88, 97, 99, 108, 111, 120, 122, 124, 132, 141, 158-159, 166-167, 169

Nielsen, Kai, 96, 185
ordination of women, 58, 114, 166
Original sin, 12, 23-24, 32, 34, 48, 80-81, 99, 106, 129, 139, 142
Osteen, Joel, 64
Packer, J I, 69
Paine, Thomas, 82
Paterson, Paige, 65
Patripassionism, 45
Paul, the Apostle, 1, 4, 122-124, 138, 141, 166, 169, 170-171, 182-184
Pentecostalism, 95
Phi Alpha Theta, 158
Pinker, Stephen, 146
Piper, John, 63
polygamy (Mormon), 112-113, 116-117
Pope John Paul II, 131
Popes, 40, 111
Prager, Dennis, 84
Prayer, 86, 89, 143, 160, 182
Predestination, 59-60, 99-100
Protestant Reformation, 59, 180
Psalm 51, 8, 13, 45
Puritans, 59
Qur'an, 111, 121
Reformed Theology, 59, 167
resurrection, 1, 2, 4, 10, 15, 17, 24, 33, 39, 42, 67, 75, 88, 97, 100, 120, 131, 139, 184
revival, 63, 147
Rosenstock-Huessy, Eugen, 3
Rosenzweig, Franz, 3
sacrifices (religious), 13, 41, 50-51, 86
Sagan, Carl, 31, 95, 173
Sanders, E P, 74, 87
Schellenberg, John, 93

Seventh-day Adventist Church, 35
Shelley, Percy Bysshe, 93-94
slavery, 115
Smith, Joseph, 74-75, 109-113, 123, 150, 157, 182
Soteriology, viii
Southern Baptist Theological Seminary, 64
Southerton, Simon G, 178
Spinoza, Baruch, 93
St Andrews, Scotland, 161
St. Anselm, 39, 83
St. Augustine, 59, 92
Stenger, Victor, 96
Stoics, 2
Stott, John, 35, 43-49, 52, 55, 68-70
Sydney Anglican Diocese, 59, 138
Telushkin, Rabbi Joseph, 85
repentance (*teshuvah*), 13, 15, 17, 34, 36, 45, 55, 83-88, 100, 155
The Enlightenment, 92, 99, 101, 118, 127-128, 148
Third Temple, 51
The Trinity, 53, 71, 73, 96, 130, 150, 158, 182
The Wonderful Wizard of Oz, 156-158
Thirty Nine Articles (Anglican), 62
Thomson, Mark D, 133, 137
Transubstantiation, 17
Tuchman, Barbara W, 29
TULIP, 60, 62
Turek, Frank, 30
Tutu, Desmond, 22
Twain, Mark, 160
Typhoon Yolanda, 105-106
Tyrannosaurus Rex, 171

Tyson, Neil deGrasse, 31
University of Newcastle, 29
Urquhart Castle, 172
Velociraptor, 171
Verdict magazine, 36
Westminster Confession of Faith, 60-62
Whitman, Walt, 162, 177
Williams, A Lukyn, 9
Witchcraft, 95
Woodruff, Wilford, 112
worship, ix, 3, 51, 64, 147-148, 155,
Wright, Robert, 96
Wright, Tom, 67
Zuckerman, Phil, 96, 146

www.ingramcontent.com/pod-product-compliance
Lightning Source LLC
Chambersburg PA
CBHW071440150426
43191CB00008B/1186